Twilio Best Practices

Learn how to build powerful real-time voice and SMS applications with Twilio

Tim Rogers

BIRMINGHAM - MUMBAI

Twilio Best Practices

Copyright © 2014 Packt Publishing

First published: December 2014

Production reference: 1151214

Published by Packt Publishing Ltd.
Livery Place
35 Livery Street
Birmingham B3 2PB, UK.

ISBN 978-1-78217-589-6

www.packtpub.com

Credits

Author
Tim Rogers

Reviewers
Shivam Dixit

Poojan Khanpara

Phil Nash

Acquisition Editor
Llewellyn Rozario

Content Development Editor
Adrian Raposo

Technical Editor
Ankur K. Ghiye

Copy Editors
Deepa Nambiar

Stuti Srivastava

Project Coordinator
Sanchita Mandal

Proofreaders
Ameesha Green

Joel T. Johnson

Indexer
Mariammal Chettiyar

Graphics
Abhinash Sahu

Production Coordinator
Arvindkumar Gupta

Cover Work
Arvindkumar Gupta

About the Author

Tim Rogers is a software engineer and student at the London School of Economics (LSE) and is from London, UK. He currently works at GoCardless, which is a payments start-up that helps businesses accept Direct Debit payments online. Here, he built the company's call center in the cloud, which is documented in a series of popular blog posts.

He also works for a number of freelance clients, helping them use the power of Twilio to do things that range from getting reviews from hotel guests to building scalable customer support operations.

In his spare time, he enjoys drinking coffee and serving in his local church and his university's Christian Union.

I would like to thank everyone at GoCardless (especially Grey Baker), all members of LSESU Christian Union, and Konnaire Scannell for their support.

About the Reviewers

Shivam Dixit is an enthusiastic web developer and a hacker. He has years of experience in both developing and breaking web applications. He actively contributes to open source projects since his participation in Google Summer of Code as a student. He is closely involved with a nonprofit organization called Open Web Application Security Project (OWASP) that makes web applications more secure. He loves to solve algorithmic problems and is a passionate, competitive programmer. You can read about his experiences on his blog at http://shivamdixit.com/ or on Twitter at @shivamd001.

> I would like to express my gratitude to my parents, my sister, Akanksha, and my brother, Vivek, for their support and inspiration.

Poojan Khanpara is a computer enthusiast and a tinkerer at heart with a knack for building cool things. He earned his Bachelor's degree in Computer Engineering from Birla Vishvakarma Mahavidyalaya College, India, and is a graduate student at the University of Texas at Dallas, USA. He has experience in a variety of fields in computer science, from designing algorithms to big data.

> I would like to thank my family and my roommates — Parth Trivedi, Rajen Patel, and Vaghesh Patel — for the incredible support they provided.

Phil Nash is a web developer who lives and works in London. He has worked in the web industry for more than 7 years, specializing in Ruby, JavaScript, and frontend development. During that time, he built web applications for products and campaigns and enjoyed rapid prototyping in Ruby on Rails. He maintains and contributes to several popular RubyGems.

Phil works as a developer evangelist for Twilio, supporting developer communities in London and around Europe. You can find him in real life attending or speaking at conferences and meetups. His writing can be found online on the Twilio blog, on Twitter as `@philnash` or at `http://philna.sh`.

www.PacktPub.com

Support files, eBooks, discount offers, and more

For support files and downloads related to your book, please visit www.PacktPub.com.

Did you know that Packt offers eBook versions of every book published, with PDF and ePub files available? You can upgrade to the eBook version at www.PacktPub.com and as a print book customer, you are entitled to a discount on the eBook copy. Get in touch with us at service@packtpub.com for more details.

At www.PacktPub.com, you can also read a collection of free technical articles, sign up for a range of free newsletters and receive exclusive discounts and offers on Packt books and eBooks.

https://www2.packtpub.com/books/subscription/packtlib

Do you need instant solutions to your IT questions? PacktLib is Packt's online digital book library. Here, you can search, access, and read Packt's entire library of books.

Why subscribe?

- Fully searchable across every book published by Packt
- Copy and paste, print, and bookmark content
- On demand and accessible via a web browser

Free access for Packt account holders

If you have an account with Packt at www.PacktPub.com, you can use this to access PacktLib today and view 9 entirely free books. Simply use your login credentials for immediate access.

Table of Contents

Preface

The Twilio platform makes it simple to integrate telephony—both calls as well as SMS and MMS messages—into your code without expensive hardware requiring a manual setup. However, getting started on such a powerful platform can be daunting.

This book will teach you how to build powerful real-time applications on the Twilio platform from start to finish, making use of phone calls and SMS messages. You'll be introduced to TwiML, the REST API, and Twilio Client before you start building two real-life applications and diving deeper into issues such as testing and security.

What this book covers

Chapter 1, *Working with TwiML*, covers TwiML, which is Twilio's XML-based language, that directs how Twilio handles incoming calls and SMSes and places outgoing calls. The actions in TwiML are called verbs, and we'll look at all of them and how they're used.

Chapter 2, *Exploring the REST API*, takes you through interacting with the data in your Twilio account, as well as placing calls and sending SMS messages. You'll learn how to set up the PHP API library, how to interact directly with the API using a tool called Postman, and how to use the API's most useful features.

Chapter 3, *Calling in the Browser with Twilio Client*, introduces Twilio Client, which is a way of making and receiving phone calls directly within your applications, in a browser or mobile app, without using a physical phone. You'll discover how this works at a high level and how to practically implement it in your code.

Chapter 4, *Twilio in the Real World*, takes you through building two real Twilio applications: a callback request tool for your website and a simple conference calling service with fully explained code samples.

Chapter 5, *Twilio in your language*, goes beyond the PHP code we've used in most of the book, showing how to download and configure Twilio's API libraries for Ruby, Python, C#, Java, Node, and Salesforce.com.

Chapter 6, *Securing your Twilio App*, helps you keep your application and Twilio credit secure with two-factor authentication on your Twilio account. We will verify that the requests you're receiving really come from Twilio and will set up a circuit breaker to detect bugs and account misuse.

Chapter 7, *Testing, Debugging, and Deploying Twilio Apps*, explains how to test your apps before you release them into the wild and then how to monitor and maintain them later using the App Monitor and Request Inspector.

Chapter 8, *Online Resources*, contains some helpful links to help you get the most from this book and follow Twilio's best practices.

What you need for this book

For this book, you'll need a computer with a text editor and a web browser. You'll also need a web server to run PHP code. You can use a paid hosting provider (see *Chapter 8*, *Online Resources*, for recommendations) or set this up on your own computer.

If you'd like to run a PHP-compatible web server on your own computer:

- On Windows, Microsoft's PHP on Windows installer is the simplest way to get started. Refer to `http://www.microsoft.com/web/platform/phponwindows.aspx`.

- On Mac OS X, PHP comes bundled with the OS but needs some simple setup. Refer to `http://php.net/manual/en/install.macosx.bundled.php` for instructions.

- On other Unix and Linux operating systems, there are a range of ways to set up PHP. Refer to `http://php.net/manual/en/install.unix.php` for a list of some of the options.

Who this book is for

If you're a developer in any programming language looking to get started with integrating Twilio into your applications, or if you're hoping to perfect your skills after already trying Twilio, then this book is for you.

This book will provides full code samples in PHP, JavaScript, and HTML, but it will be useful no matter what language you choose to use, showing you how to structure your applications, plus how and where to interact with Twilio.

Conventions

In this book, you will find a number of styles of text that distinguish between different kinds of information. Here are some examples of these styles, and an explanation of their meaning.

Code words in text, database table names, folder names, filenames, file extensions, pathnames, dummy URLs, user input, and Twitter handles are shown as follows: "The `<Play>` verb lets you play audio."

A block of code is set as follows:

```
<?xml version="1.0" encoding="UTF-8"?>
<Response>
<Say>Twilio Best Practices is number one!</Say>
</Response>
```

When we wish to draw your attention to a particular part of a code block, the relevant lines or items are set in bold:

```
<p>
   access this conference, participants should dial
   <your phone number here> and use access code {{
   $conference->access_code }}.
 </p>
```

Any command-line input or output is written as follows:

```
composer require "watson/validating:0.10.*"
```

New terms and **important words** are shown in bold. Words that you see on the screen, in menus or dialog boxes for example, appear in the text like this: "Once you've got your number, head back to the **Numbers** screen and click on the one you've just bought."

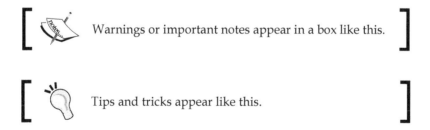

Warnings or important notes appear in a box like this.

Tips and tricks appear like this.

Reader feedback

Feedback from our readers is always welcome. Let us know what you think about this book—what you liked or may have disliked. Reader feedback is important for us to develop titles that you really get the most out of.

To send us general feedback, simply send an e-mail to feedback@packtpub.com, and mention the book title via the subject of your message.

If there is a topic that you have expertise in and you are interested in either writing or contributing to a book, see our author guide on www.packtpub.com/authors.

Customer support

Now that you are the proud owner of a Packt book, we have a number of things to help you to get the most from your purchase.

Downloading the example code

You can download the example code files for all Packt books you have purchased from your account at http://www.packtpub.com. If you purchased this book elsewhere, you can visit http://www.packtpub.com/support and register to have the files e-mailed directly to you.

Errata

Although we have taken every care to ensure the accuracy of our content, mistakes do happen. If you find a mistake in one of our books—maybe a mistake in the text or the code—we would be grateful if you would report this to us. By doing so, you can save other readers from frustration and help us improve subsequent versions of this book. If you find any errata, please report them by visiting http://www.packtpub.com/submit-errata, selecting your book, clicking on the **Errata Submission Form** link, and entering the details of your errata. Once your errata are verified, your submission will be accepted and the errata will be uploaded on our website, or added to any list of existing errata, under the Errata section of that title. Any existing errata can be viewed by selecting your title from http://www.packtpub.com/support.

To view the previously submitted errata, go to https://www.packtpub.com/books/content/support and enter the name of the book in the search field. The required information will appear under the Errata section.

Piracy

Piracy of copyright material on the Internet is an ongoing problem across all media. At Packt, we take the protection of our copyright and licenses very seriously. If you come across any illegal copies of our works, in any form, on the Internet, please provide us with the location address or website name immediately so that we can pursue a remedy.

Please contact us at copyright@packtpub.com with a link to the suspected pirated material.

We appreciate your help in protecting our authors, and our ability to bring you valuable content.

Questions

You can contact us at questions@packtpub.com if you are having a problem with any aspect of the book, and we will do our best to address it.

1
Working with TwiML

TwiML is a Twilio-specific XML-based language that is used within a Twilio application to describe what Twilio should do when an incoming call or message hits one of your Twilio phone numbers. TwiML is our way of asking Twilio to *do things*. Therefore, it's fitting that the XML elements we use are called **verbs**. For example, we have verbs such as Play, Dial, Record, and Gather, and they are accompanied by **nouns** such as Number, Client, and Conference.

In this chapter, you will learn the following topics:

- What TwiML is
- How TwiML fits into your Twilio application
- How to set up an inbound phone number
- The data you get from Twilio for inbound calls
- How to use all of the TwiML verbs including `<Play>`, `<Gather>`, and `<Dial>`
- Best practices and tips for working with TwiML

Where in my application will I be using TwiML?

In our Twilio account, we can buy phone numbers which are attached to to a particular URL. Twilio will make a `GET` or `POST` request to that URL, in order to fetch TwiML when there's an inbound call or message. The TwiML we return tells Twilio what to do in response to the call or **Short Message Service** (**SMS**).

When something happens with our phone number—namely an inbound call or incoming SMS—Twilio sends us a **webhook** that tells us about what's going on and allows us to direct what happens.

We'll also use TwiML when we place outbound calls using Twilio's **REST API**. To make a call, we have to specify the URL for a piece of TwiML that will handle that call. Once the dialed party picks up, Twilio will go through that markup, perhaps playing a message or recording its input. As part of its webhooks, Twilio provides information such as the number called and the phone number of the caller in the headers. This means you can customize what you ask Twilio to do based on a variety of different data points related to the call.

For instance, by constructing the right TwiML, you can ask Twilio's text-to-speech engine to read some text, play an MP3, dial a call, and many other things.

You can serve up your TwiML from whichever framework, language, and web server you're using. In my examples, I'll use PHP, but it's equally possible to work in the same way in Ruby (on Rails) or any other language.

PHP makes building powerful and dynamic TwiML very simple, as we can easily change the outputted XML using familiar control structures, such as `if` and `else`, which are embedded right on our page.

If you're using a PHP framework, such as Laravel or Cake, or a similar one in other languages, such as Ruby's Ruby on Rails, you'll be able to build XML templates using your usual templating library just as you would for HTML pages.

Getting started with TwiML

To set the URLs that Twilio will webhook for incoming calls and SMSes, log in to your Twilio account and choose **Numbers** from the navigation bar on top of the screen, as shown in the following screenshot:.

If you haven't already, you'll want to buy a phone number. Twilio makes this really easy. You just click on **Buy a number**, which is on the right-hand side, choose your country, and then pick a number of your choice.

Most numbers cost just $1 per month, so cost isn't a huge barrier. Many countries' numbers will support both calls and SMSes, but this is not always the case. Twilio will always tell you what capabilities are supported as part of the buying process.

Once you've got your number, head back to the **Numbers** screen and click on the one you've just bought.

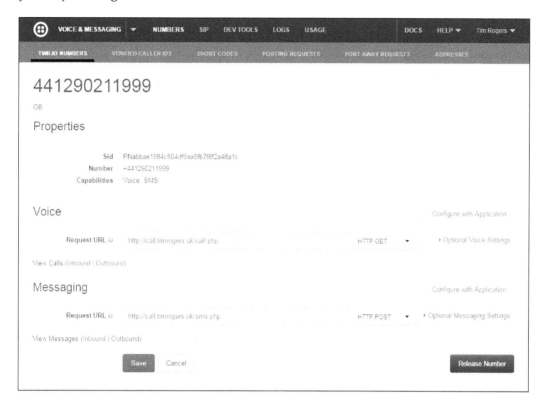

You'll see that this screen is split into two key sections: **Voice** and **Messaging**. You can set separate URLs and HTTP methods for each section. If you're working in PHP, you can usually safely use either GET or POST, but some frameworks and languages will have more specific requirements.

If you click on the optional settings using the link on the right-hand side, you will see a few advanced options which we'll cover. We'll do the same with the powerful **Configure with Application** setting.

Let's write two quick *hello world* TwiML snippets, in keeping with programming tradition, using PHP. Start by creating a file called call.php as follows:

```
<?xml version="1.0" encoding="UTF-8"?>
<Response>
  <Say>Hello world. We love you guys in
  <?php echo $_GET['FromCountry']; ?>.</Say>
</Response>
```

In the preceding sample, you'll see that this PHP responds with some XML. XML as a language is very similar to HTML, so it'll look familiar. If you haven't encountered it previously, don't worry; you'll get the hang of it over the course of this chapter.

Inside the <Response> block where Twilio looks to find what it should do in response to the incoming call, we use the <Say> verb. The text we put within the <Say> element is what Twilio's text-to-speech engine will speak.

We're already taking advantage of PHP here by looking at some GET data that Twilio provides with the request. In this case, the voice is going to say the name of the country where the caller is located — FromCountry. There are lots of other great things you can do, which we'll cover later.

After the <Say> verb, Twilio will hang up, as it has nothing more to do.

We've now written a handler for incoming calls, so let's also write one for SMSes. We can do something very similar indeed; let's save this as message.php:

```
<?xml version="1.0" encoding="UTF-8"?>
<Response>
  <Message>Hello world. We love you guys in
  <?php echo $_GET['FromCountry']; ?>.</Message>
</Response>
```

As you'll see, we do exactly the same thing here except for using the <Message> verb instead of the <Say> verb. This means that we'll text the sender with the message rather than saying it to them over the phone. We'll cover the <Message> verb in more detail later.

You'll now need to upload these PHP files somewhere where they can be accessed by Twilio. You'll probably have some hosting set up, but if you do not, there are a range of great options. I've included a few recommendations in *Chapter 8, Online Resources*.

Alternatively, you can use a local server; see my tip on using a great tool called **ngrok** at the end of the chapter for help with this.

Now that we've set up those PHP files, add the URLs of your call.php and message.php files to your Twilio number, and then hit **Save**.

Let's see the magic happen. Try calling and SMSing your number. First, Twilio webhooks our TwiML URL, letting our code know about the call and asking it what to do. We respond with TwiML such that Twilio speaks out loud our "hello world" message if we're calling in, or SMSes it to us if we've sent in a text. You've now seen the power of TwiML.

Digging deeper – Twilio's requests

In the preceding example, you've seen that Twilio includes some helpful data in its request when it hits your server to fetch the TwiML it needs in order to handle an incoming call or message.

We pulled out the country where the caller is located, which is stored in the FromCountry parameter. We grabbed this in PHP using $_GET, but you can do the same in any web language.

Alongside the caller's location, Twilio includes a whole lot of useful information.

Here are the highlights:

Parameter	What it means
CallSid/MessageSid	This refers to the unique reference for this call or message, as appropriate.
	This can be particularly useful to store in a database if you might want to look up this call using the REST API later.
From	This refers to the caller's phone number in the international format (for example, +, then the country code, and then the local number).
To	This tells you which of your Twilio phone numbers is being dialed in the international format, as described previously.
CallStatus	This tells you about the current status of the call, which may be queued, ringing, in-progress, completed, busy, failed or no-answer.
ApiVersion	This refers to the Twilio API version being used for this call; you can safely ignore this parameter.
Direction	This refers to the direction—or in some sense, the type—of call in progress. This will be inbound for incoming calls, outbound-api for calls initiated with the REST API (we'll learn more about this in *Chapter 2, Exploring REST API*) and outbound-dial for calls initiated from the TwiML <Dial> verb.
ForwardedFrom	For some forwarded calls, this will include the number from which the call was forwarded, but this is not supported by all carriers.

Parameter		What it means
CallerName		Twilio allows you to enable caller ID lookup on your phone numbers for $0.01 per lookup. If you've enabled this, this will contain the caller's name if a result was found.
From/To	City	This refers to the city where the caller/number being called is located (this will not necessarily be provided).
	State	This refers to the state, province, or country where the caller/number being called is located (this will not necessarily be provided).
	Zip	This refers to the zip or postal code of the caller/number being called (this will not necessarily be provided).
	Country	This refers to the country where the caller/number being called is located
Body		This refers to the text received in the SMS (SMS only).

This data, which Twilio provides, can help you implement a wide range of dynamic features into your TwiML, such as the following:

- Changing how the call is handled depending on the number being called
- Switching languages based on the location of the caller
- Responding to what someone actually said in an SMS

 Further details are available in Twilio's comprehensive documentation at
`https://www.twilio.com/docs/api/twiml/twilio_request`

The world of TwiML verbs

Verbs are the belt and braces of your TwiML. They're the part that actually tells Twilio what it should do when a call comes in or a text arrives.

I'll seek to give you an introduction to what you'll be looking at while using each verb. For more specific details, you'll want to directly refer to the documentation.

Twilio's documentation is pretty exhaustive and is available online at `https://www.twilio.com/docs/api/twiml/`

<Say>

The `<Say>` verb invokes Twilio's text-to-speech engine, that is, it gets Twilio to say things:

```xml
<?xml version="1.0" encoding="UTF-8"?>
<Response>
  <Say>Twilio Best Practices is number one!</Say>
</Response>
```

Inside the `<Say>` tag, you provide the text that you want it to speak. In Twilio parlance, what's nested inside the verb is called the **noun**. In this case, it's just plain text, but for many verbs, it'll be further XML tags.

By setting attributes on the `<Say>` verb, we can switch the voice from male to female and can also change the language of our text. The full options are in Twilio's documentation, but it works along these lines:

```xml
<?xml version="1.0" encoding="UTF-8"?>
<Response>
  <Say voice="alice" language="fr-FR">J'adore ce livre -
  c'est le meilleur livre que j'ai jamais lu!</Say>
</Response>
```

In our `<Say>` verb, we can specify a range of attributes that customize what happens:

Attribute	What it means
voice	This sets the voice we want to use while speaking our text; this can be set to man, woman, or alice. The voice you choose affects the options available for the language attribute.
loop	How many times should our message be read out? If this is not set, the message will not be repeated. Set it to 0 to make it loop forever, or set a specific number of loops.
language	This sets the language that your message is in. For the man and woman voice, American English, British English, Spanish, French, German, and Italian are available, but the alice voice supports many more languages. It defaults to en (that is, American English). For more details, see `https://www.twilio.com/docs/api/twiml/say#attributes-manwoman`

There are a few quirks that are worth noting with the <Say> verb. Take a look:

- As we can construct our TwiML with PHP, it's easy to dynamically generate the text that is spoken, as we did in call.php earlier in the chapter.

- Always test your <Say> verbs well by calling in yourself. Twilio might not always pronounce things perfectly, and you should be especially careful to check the annunciation of numbers, dates, and amounts of money:

    ° A great example is that if we include 1234 — for instance, as a PIN number or password, Twilio will say *one thousand two hundred and thirty four*, rather than *one two three four*. If we wanted it to say the latter, we should write 1 2 3 4, with a space between each number, perhaps also using a <Pause> verb between numbers to keep it from being read too fast.

    ° With proper nouns, such as place names or products, you might need to be creative in order to have proper pronunciation. One way to do this is to spell things phonetically.

<Play>

The <Play> verb lets you play audio. This is useful for things such as holding music and using your own voiceovers where text-to-speech just seems a little too awkward:

```
<?xml version="1.0" encoding="UTF-8"?>
<Response>
  <Play>https://s3.amazonaws.com/twilio-best-
  practices/hello.mp3</Play>
</Response>
```

Inside the <Play> tag, provide the URL of the audio file to be played. Twilio supports a number of formats, but you'll almost certainly want to use either MP3 or WAV.

You can also use the <Play> verb to play DTMF tones (that is, the sound made when you press a number on your phone's keypad) to test other phone systems. We won't cover this, as it's very much an edge use case.

As with the <Say> verb, the loop attribute is supported; it works exactly the same as for <Say>, allowing us to repeat our audio clip as many times as we need or forever.

The most important caveat to remember with <Play> is that Twilio will cache the audio file you provide. This means that changing voiceovers or hold music is not necessarily as simple as just changing the file where they're stored.

At the same time, Twilio's caching is useful because it will help you save bandwidth and, therefore, cost as well—especially if you're hosting your audio with a provider such as Amazon S3 (http://aws.amazon.com/s3/)

Twilio will obey the standard HTTP cache headers to decide when to re-download your audio file and when to keep using a copy it has used previously; see https://www.twilio.com/help/faq/voice/how-can-i-change-the-cache-behavior-of-audio-files for details. So, to change audio files, you'll need to do one of the following:

- Wait for the caching period to finish
- Re-deploy your application, pointing to a fresh URL for the audio (for instance, uploading your audio files into directories named with the date of the application version, and then updating all the references in your TwiML)

<Pause>

The <Pause> verb waits silently for a specified number of seconds, or one second by default. It's simply used like this, with the length of time for waiting specified in the length attribute:

```
<Pause length="5" />
```

> Note that the <Pause> verb looks a little different than any other verb because it uses a self-closing tag. It has no noun(s), but it takes an attribute that represents the number of seconds for which you wish to wait. As we'll see later, the <Reject> verb works in a very similar way.

<Gather>

The <Gather> verb allows you to take input from a caller by asking them to enter digits on their phone's keypad. This allows you to build complex, interactive applications.

The <Gather> verb is slightly more complicated to use than the verbs we've seen so far, as you will be nesting other verbs inside it.

So, for example, we might nest a <Say> verb inside our <Gather> block to say a message and then wait for the caller's input.

In this example, we say a message and then wait for 10 seconds for the caller to enter a single digit in response:

```
<?xml version="1.0" encoding="UTF-8"?>
<Response>
  <Gather timeout="10" numDigits="1" action="digits.php">
```

```
    <Say>Choose an option from the menu. Press 1 for sales. Press 2 for
    customer services. Press 3 for billing.</Say>
    </Gather>
  <Say>You didn't enter an option. Goodbye.</Say>
  </Response>
```

Once a customer has entered a digit, Twilio will make a POST request to the action, which is `digits.php`, including the digits that the customer entered in the `Digits` parameter. This allows you to build awesome interactive applications. Here's an example of what we can do in `digits.php`:

```
<?xml version="1.0" encoding="UTF-8"?>
<Response>
  <?php if ($_POST['Digits'] == "1") { ?>
    <Say>Please wait - we'll put you through now.</Say>
  <Dial>
    ...
  </Dial>
  <?php } else { ?>
    <Say>Our phone lines are currently closed - please drop us
    an email at support@twiliobestpractices.com.</Say>
  <?php } ?>
</Response>
```

Inside our `<Gather>` block, we can nest not only `<Play>` verbs, but also `<Say>` and `<Pause>`.

Here, we first check whether the digit 1 has been entered. If it has, we ask Twilio to say a message, and then we add another action afterwards. Here, we use a `<Dial>` verb through which we might add the caller to a queue or dial to them through to a particular number.

If a number other than 1 was entered, we play an alternative message.

 When you're using `<Gather>`, always test all of the paths through your call flow. This means that you try every option; otherwise, it's easy to not pick up serious errors with your application.

<Record>

Unsurprisingly, the `<Record>` verb lets you record the caller's voice. This is perfect for things such as building a voicemail service, registering participants' names for a conference call, or gathering feedback from users:

```
<Record timeout="30" transcribe="true" action="/recording.php" />
```

In the preceding code snippet, we record for up to 30 seconds, ask Twilio to try to transcribe the audio into text, and then Twilio makes a POST request to recording. php with the URL of the recorded audio as an MP3.

 Note that using Twilio's transcription feature costs $0.05 cents per minute transcribed.

Twilio will expect recording.php to also return TwiML in order to let it know what to do next. For instance, you might hang up the call or even play back the caller's recording to them for them to check and confirm.

As you're given the recording URL, it's really easy to do all of this and much more, such as storing our recording in a database:

```php
<?php
  $recordingUrl = $_POST['RecordingUrl'];
  $transcriptionText = $_POST['TranscriptionText'];
  $callSid = $_POST['CallSid']; // The unique identifier
  for this call
  // Save $recordingUrl to a database against $callSid, and then…
?>
<?xml version="1.0" encoding="UTF-8"?>
<Response>
  <Say>Thank you - here's the message we just recorded:</Say>
  <Play><?php echo $recordingUrl; ?></Play>
  <Say>Thank you, and goodbye.</Say>
  <Hangup />
</Response>
```

In the preceding code snippet, we take some of the data provided by Twilio in the request (that is, in $_POST) and store it to variables in order to use it later. We then use this to form a TwiML response, which plays a message and then plays the caller's recording back to them. It then says goodbye and hangs up.

 The <Record> verb doesn't support nesting. If you want to record an entire call, which is probably the primary example where you'll want to do something else, the flow is slightly different and forms part of what we'll do with the <Dial> verb. We'll cover this later.

<Message>

The `<Message>` verb allows you send a text or **Multimedia Messaging Service (MMS)** message as part of a phone call's flow. Using this verb is simple. On a basic level, you just nest plain text within it, representing the message that should be sent:

```
<?xml version="1.0" encoding="UTF-8"?>
<Response>
  <Message>Thanks for calling - if you need anything else,
  just let us know.</Message>
</Response>
```

> **Downloading the example code**
> You can download the example code fies for all Packt books you have purchased from your account at http://www.packtpub.com. If you purchased this book elsewhere, you can visit http://www.packtpub.com/support and register to have the files e-mailed directly to you.

Twilio will automagically, if nothing else is specified, send a text to the current caller with the caller ID as the number that is being called.

Of course, you might want to text someone else. For example, imagine that we have a fault-reporting service where we'll text an available engineer when someone reports a problem:

```php
<?php
  $engineerPhoneNumber = "+441290211999";
?>
<?xml version="1.0" encoding="UTF-8"?>
<Response>
  <Say>Thanks for letting us know about this fault - someone
  will call you back very shortly.</Say>
  <Message To="<?php echo $engineerPhoneNumber; ?>">A caller
  just reported a fault. Please call them back on <?php
  echo $_POST['From']; ?>.</Message>
</Response>
```

Here, we play a message to the caller and then send a text to a provided phone number (stored in the `$engineerPhoneNumber` PHP variable) with the caller's phone number.

> Most of the time, this won't be necessary, but we can set up a **status callback** (`statusCallback`) on the `<Message>` verb to have our application notified as to whether an SMS was successfully sent. For details, see Twilio's documentation at https://www.twilio.com/docs/api/twiml/sms/message.

Using the `<Message>` verb, we can also send MMS messages with included images. In order to do this, we'll nest a `<Media>` noun with a URL pointing to an image inside our `<Message>` verb. To include an image *and* text, we can nest a `<Media>` noun and a `<Body>` noun as follows:

```xml
<?xml version="1.0" encoding="UTF-8"?>
<Response>
  <Message>
    <Media>https://demo.twilio.com/owl.png</Media>
    <Body>Owls are excellent.</Body>
  </Message>
</Response>
```

 At the moment, MMS messaging is only available with select Twilio phone numbers in the US and Canada, but this will expand in due course.

If you're not interested in sending messages as part of a call, don't worry; we'll cover how to send outbound SMSes via the REST API on an ad-hoc basis in the next chapter.

<Enqueue>

As part of offering a full suite for building phone services, Twilio supports the queuing functionality that is very popular for use in call centers and similar applications.

Simply nest the name of a queue that the caller should be joined to within the verb:

```xml
<?xml version="1.0" encoding="UTF-8"?>
<Response>
  <Say>Please wait and one of our team members will be with
  you shortly.</Say>
  <Enqueue>Support</Enqueue>
</Response>
```

On the `<Enqueue>` verb, we can specify a `waitUrl` attribute. This should point to a TwiML that will be repeatedly run through for the caller while they wait in the queue.

This will default to play hold music provided by Twilio, but we can add our own, or even read the caller's position in the queue to them when we specify our own custom file. We can set our own waiting TwiML like this:

```xml
<Enqueue waitUrl="waiting.php">Support</Enqueue>
```

Follow this up by writing your own `waiting.php` file like this:

```xml
<?xml version="1.0" encoding="UTF-8"?>
<Response>
  <Play>http://com.twilio.sounds.music.s3.amazonaws.com/
  ClockworkWaltz.mp3</Play>
  <Say>You are currently in position <?php echo
  $_POST['QueuePosition']; ?> in the queue.</Say>
</Response>
```

Here, we play some of Twilio's wait music (you can see a list of their provided tracks at `http://s3.amazonaws.com/com.twilio.sounds.music/index.xml`) and then play the caller's position in the queue back to them.

> From our `waitUrl` attribute, most TwiML verbs (except `<Dial>` verb) are supported. This means that you can do a range of things in the wait process, from playing a message like we did previously to collecting details from the customer with the `<Gather>` verb.

A call can be dequeued in three ways:

- By another caller being connected to the call through the `<Dial>` verb's `<Queue>` noun
- Via the REST API
- With the `<Leave>` verb

We'll cover these in detail later, but for now, let's take a look at the `<Leave>` verb.

`<Leave>`

This verb is a very simple one. It is used from a queue's `waitUrl` (see the preceding section), and it lets us remove the caller from the queue and run some alternative TwiML instead.

As a crude example, let's add a caller to our support queue but add a `we're now closed`-style message after our `<Enqueue>` verb:

```xml
<?xml version="1.0" encoding="UTF-8"?>
<Response>
  <Say>Please wait and one of our team member will
  be with you shortly.</Say>
  <Enqueue waitUrl="waiting.php">Support</Enqueue>
  <Say>We're now closed – please call back tomorrow.</Say>
  <Hangup />
</Response>
```

Once the caller is joined to the *Support* queue, the execution of our TwiML document will be stopped and Twilio will loop over the TwiML in `waiting.php`, waiting for the call to be dequeued instead.

Only if and when the caller leaves this queue will we continue to execute our TwiML so that the `<Say>` block gets run.

We might want to remove callers from the queue at 6 p.m. when our customer support lines close. Lets write some TwiML in `waiting.php` with the help of a little PHP. To do this, take a look at the following code:

```
<?xml version="1.0" encoding="UTF-8"?>
<Response>
  <?php if (intval(date("H")) >= 18) { ?><Leave />
  <?php } else { ?>
  <Play>http://com.twilio.sounds.music.s3.amazonaws.com/
  ClockworkWaltz.mp3</Play>
    <Say>You are currently in position <?php echo
    $_POST['QueuePosition']; ?> in the queue.</Say>
  <?php } ?>
</Response>
```

Here, we check whether the hour on a 24-hour clock is more than `18` (that is, 6 p.m.). If it is, we leave the queue (so that our final bit of TwiML in the previous snippet gets run), or else, we play some hold music and then announce the caller's current position. `waiting.php` will simply be requested again and again while a caller queues.

For `<Leave>`, we can use a self-closing tag because this verb is never used with a noun. We can write `<Leave></Leave>`, which would be equivalent to `<Leave />`, but simply writing `<Leave />` is quicker.

<Dial>

The `<Dial>` verb is probably the most important and, equally, the most complex of all the TwiML verbs.

It allows us to place outbound calls and bridge them to our current one, enabling tonnes of powerful applications, from connecting inbound calls to customer support staff to setting up conferences.

For example, as part of a call, we might dial in to one of our support staff:

```xml
<?xml version="1.0" encoding="UTF-8"?>
<Response>
  <Say>Please wait while we connect you to one of customer support
  team. Please note that calls will be recorded.</Say>
  <Dial record="record-from-answer" action="recording.php">
    <Number>+441290211999</Number>
  </Dial>
</Response>
```

Here, we play a message and then call our customer support phone number, recording the call from the time it's answered and asking Twilio to post the recording to `recording.php`. When our `<Dial>` verb has an action, as is the case here, no TwiML verbs after it will be accessible (that is, used), as Twilio will move on to the action URL.

As always, Twilio has sensible defaults for the `<Dial>` verb, which can be customized. For instance, it'll set a timeout of ringing for 30 seconds before it gives up, and `callerId` will be set to the number of the current caller. You can discover all of the options in Twilio's documentation at `https://www.twilio.com/docs/api/twiml/dial`.

When you're using `<Dial>`, what you nest within it is very important. You've already seen the use of `<Number>`, which will call the number of a physical (that is, PSTN) phone. There are a number of nouns you can nest under it in order to make different kinds of calls:

<Number>

The `<Number>` noun lets you call a traditional phone number; nest one or more these under your `<Dial>` verb in order to call it.

One of the most interesting features here is that you can actually try multiple phone numbers. For example, imagine a situation, such as in the following code sample, where you want to try multiple numbers for your customer support phone line:

```xml
<?xml version="1.0" encoding="UTF-8"?>
<Response>
  <Say>Please wait while we connect you to one of the customer support
  team. Please note that calls will be recorded.</Say>
  <Dial record="record-from-answer" action="recording.php">
    <Number>+441290211999</Number>
    <Number>+441290211998</Number>
```

```
    </Dial>
    <!—Let's hang up when the dialled call is over --!>
    <Hangup />
</Response>
```

With this TwiML, Twilio will attempt to call both of the numbers. As soon as someone picks up, it'll stop trying the other.

The `<Number>` noun also provides some advanced functionality that lets you control what happens when the dialed party has answered the call, such as the `sendDigits` and `url` attributes:

- With `sendDigits`, you can ask Twilio to send some DTMF tones to a called party when they pick up (for example, to reach a particular extension behind that number).

- With `url`, you can specify the URL or path to a piece of TwiML that can be run against the caller before they're connected to the current call.

Let's go through examples of both of those options.

First, we'll look at `url`; we'll start with our TwiML for the actually incoming call, just like we did previously:

```
<?xml version="1.0" encoding="UTF-8"?>
<Response>
  <Say>Please wait while we connect you to one of customer support
  team. Please note that calls will be recorded.</Say>
  <Dial record="record-from-answer" action="recording.php">
    <Number url="intro.php">+441290211999</Number>
    <Number url="intro.php">+441290211998</Number>
  </Dial>
  <!—Let's hang up when the dialed call is over --!>
  <Hangup />
</Response>
```

A `intro.php` file will be played to our customer support agents once they've picked up the call but before the call is actually connected through, letting them reject the call if it's inconvenient:

```
<?xml version="1.0" encoding="UTF-8"?>
<Response>
  <Gather timeout="5" action="digits.php" numDigits="1">
    <Say>This is an incoming customer support call – press any key
    on your phone in the next 5 seconds to accept the call, or
    otherwise hang up.</Say>
  </Gather>
  <Hangup />
</Response>
```

We'll play a message to the customer support agent and then wait for their input. If they press a digit at the prompt, we'll move on to the `digits.php` TwiML file. Otherwise, the call will be rejected and thus hung up, leaving Twilio to keep trying the other number in the `<Dial>` block.

Lastly, we'll need to create a `digits.php` file to deal with the called party's input:

```
<?xml version="1.0" encoding="UTF-8"?>
<Response>
  <Say>Thanks - you'll now be connected.</Say>
</Response>
```

The agent will be played a quick message, and then Twilio will actually connect the dialed party to the original call.

 You'll notice that we need to do nothing to make this bridging of the two calls happen; it's just that in this context, Twilio's default behavior does this when there is no more TwiML left.

The `sendDigits` attribute is useful when we want to dial some digits once the called party picks up. This is useful for automating other phone menus and services, or for dialing an extension, as follows:

```
<?xml version="1.0" encoding="UTF-8"?>
<Response>
  <Dial record="record-from-answer" action="recording.php">
    <Number sendDigits="wwwww100">+441290211999</Number>
  </Dial>
</Response>
```

Here, we'll dial our number, but when they pick up, we'll wait for 2.5 seconds (each `w` character represents a half-second pause) and then dial `100`, our imaginary extension.

<Sip>

Apart from dialing through to physical phones, we can also make calls on Twilio over **Session Initiation Protocol** (**SIP**). SIP is a standard, or perhaps *the standard* for Internet telephony, connecting together a range of phone networks.

The `<Sip>` verb effectively acts as a cheaper complement to making calls over PSTN using the `<Number>` noun at less than half the cost of calling a US phone number.

We'd dial a SIP URI (which identifies a particular client on a particular SIP server) as follows:

```xml
<?xml version="1.0" encoding="UTF-8"?>
<Response>
  <Dial record="record-from-answer" action="recording.php">
    <Sip>sip:me@timrogers.uk</Sip>
  </Dial>
</Response>
```

The `<Sip>` verb works with all of the various `<Dial>` verb options we've seen previously for calls using the `<Number>` noun. For example, we can ask to record calls or set a timeout from the `<Dial>` verb.

The URL attribute is also available on the `<Sip>` noun and works in exactly the same way as it works for `<Number>`, letting us add call screening and other such features with ease.

 We can even combine calls to different kinds of destinations under one `<Dial>` verb. For instance, we can simultaneously try to call a member of the staff's mobile phone and the SIP phone on their desk by nesting `<Sip>` and `<Number>` nouns under a `<Dial>` verb.

There are lots of niche options available to you when you're working with SIP in Twilio that aren't worth covering in this book; examples include, forcing the TCP or UDP transport for the connection and sending custom headers with the SIP request.

 You can read about these and other customizations at https://www.twilio.com/docs/api/twiml/sip.

SIP authentication

Often, SIP servers will have authentication on them to prevent unwanted calls. This will usually work in one of two ways: username and password or IP whitelisting.

Username and password protection

As part of our `<Sip>` noun, we can specify a username and password that Twilio should provide when sending the INVITE message to the SIP server. To do this, we simply use the `username` and `password` attributes on the noun as follows:

```xml
<Sip username="twilio"
password="twiliorocks">sip:me@timrogers.uk</Sip>
```

Working with IP whitelisting

Perhaps a more common (but harder to deal with) form of authentication is IP whitelisting. This is where you'll set up your SIP server to only accept inbound calls from certain IP ranges.

Fortunately, Twilio provides you with a list of the IP addresses from which the SIP traffic may come. You can find them at the bottom of the page at `https://www.twilio.com/docs/sip`.

You should revisit this page from time to time, as Twilio expects to add additional IPs to enhance *scalability* and *reliability* in future.

<Client>

Twilio's `<Client>` allows you to include voice capabilities within a web page or native app. This means that people can make and take calls from their own devices without using the legacy telephony networks or complicated SIP setups.

This makes it easy to build powerful telephony solutions, for example, browser-to-browser calling within a web application. However, part of the magic is that it's fully connected to the rest of Twilio's platform.

This means that we can set up Twilio Client in a browser and then take incoming calls to it over a traditional phone number. Twilio Client uses TwiML in exactly the same ways as we've already seen for both incoming and outbound calls.

By way of an example, you can imagine a phone conferencing service that uses this to enhance its functionality. Attendees and presenters on a call will be able to join in either through their browser using a headset, from their mobile phone via a custom app, or from any phone of their choice on a local phone number. All of this can be run through Twilio.

Each individual connected to Twilio with Twilio Client will have their own **client identifier**. It's unique within the scope of our Twilio account and is what we use to connect calls to a particular user. Connecting to a particular client within the context of a `<Dial>` verb is very simple indeed:

```xml
<?xml version="1.0" encoding="UTF-8"?>
<Response>
  <Dial record="record-from-answer" action="recording.php">
    <Client>the-client-identifier</Client>
  </Dial>
</Response>
```

If Twilio Client sounds great, you're in luck. Refer to *Chapter 3, Calling in the Browser with Twilio Client.*

<Conference>

Using Twilio, we can easily build our own custom phone conferencing tool to rival commercial alternatives.

Doing this is a great option as Twilio's APIs give you the power to perform all sorts of integrations and customizations. The `<Conference>` verb is really quite a complex noun as it allows you to wield almost all of the features you'd see in professional conferencing tools from your own code.

The `<Conference>` noun creates or adds a caller to a conference room of your choice. Simply use the noun and place the name of a room inside it. You don't have to create it ahead of time:

```xml
<?xml version="1.0" encoding="UTF-8"?>
<Response>
  <Dial>
    <Conference>Monday Morning Meeting</Conference>
  </Dial>
</Response>
```

Let's quickly cover the different options — there are a lot of them — and then dive into an example:

Option	How it works?
muted	Set this to `true` or `false` to determine whether this caller can speak to others in the conference, or if they can only listen in. This is set to `false` by default.
beep	This specifies whether this person being added to the conference should hear a beep when people join or leave the conference room.
	It defaults to `true`, but it can be turned off with `false` or set to happen only `onEnter` or `onExit`.
startConferenceOnEnter	This determines whether the conference starts when this caller enters the call (provided there is another participant in the room as well).
	This defaults to `true`, but you might wish to set it to `false` for some callers if, for instance, you want a conference to only start once the presenter arrives.

Option	How it works?
endConferenceOnExit	This sets whether this conference stops once this caller exits. It defaults to `false`, but if set to `true`, when this caller leaves, all other participants will be forced out.
waitUrl	This allows you to specify a TwiML URL that will be looped while the current caller waits for another participant to join the room if they're the first to join.
	By default, Twilio will play some rather horrible music, but by providing the URL of your own TwiML, you can add your own music or messages.
waitMethod	This allows you to set the HTTP method with which the `waitUrl` TwiML will be requested to either `GET` or `POST`.
maxParticipants	This sets the maximum number of participants that will be allowed in this conference, defaulting to `40` (the maximum ever allowed by Twilio).
record	This specifies whether this conference should be recorded. It defaults to `do-not-record`, but it can be set to `record-from-start` in order to make a recording.
	The recording's URL will be fired over to `eventCallbackUrl` once the conference is over.
trim	This specifies whether the conference's recording should have silence at the beginning or end of the conference trimmed off. It defaults to `trim-silence`, but it can be disabled by setting it to `do-not-trim`.
eventCallbackUrl	This is the relative or absolute URL that will receive a `POST` request when the conference is over, with a `RecordingUrl` pointing to a recording of the conference if recording is enabled with the `record` parameter.

Let's build a basic conference where we'll have a passcode for presenters and a passcode for attendees. First, we'll create a TwiML file to handle incoming calls:

```xml
<?xml version="1.0" encoding="UTF-8"?>
<Response>
  <Gather timeout="10" action="digits.php" numDigits="6">
    <Say>Enter your six digit pass code to join
    the conference.<Say>
  </Gather>
  <Hangup />
</Response>
```

This file will play a message and wait for 10 seconds for the caller to enter a six-digit code.

If they fail to enter the code, we'll hang up. In the real world, we'd probably want to do something nicer than this. Otherwise, we'll make a POST request to digits.php with the Digits parameter containing what was entered on the keypad. Let's create the digits.php file:

```php
<?php
$presenterCode = "123456";
$attendeeCode = "654321";
?>
<?xml version="1.0" encoding="UTF-8"?>
<Response>
<?php if ($_POST['Digits'] == $presenterCode) { ?>
  <Say>Thank you, presenter. We'll connect you now.</Say>
  <Dial>
    <Conference endConferenceOnExit ="true">Room</Conference>
  </Dial>
<?php } else if ($_POST['Digits'] == $attendeeCode) { ?>
  <Say>Thank you - we'll add you to the conference now. You'll
  hear hold music until a presenter joins.</Say>
  <Dial>
    <Conference startConferenceOnEnter="false">Room</Conference>
  </Dial>
<?php } else { ?>
  <Say>Sorry, that conference doesn't exist. Goodbye.</Say>
  <Hangup />
<?php } ?>
</Response>
```

Here, we've got a fair bit of logic to go through:

- In the first couple of lines, we set our conference passcodes:
    - In the real world, we'd want to connect this to a database that can handle our different conference code, amongst other things.

- If the caller enters the presenter code, which is 123456, we add them to the conference. By default, the conference will be able to start when they join (as soon as there is another attendee there), but we customize the endConferenceOnExit option so that the conference finishes the moment they leave.

- If the caller enters the attendee code, which is 654321, we play a message to them and add them to the conference. However, we customize the startConferenceOnEnter option so that the conference can never start until there is at least one presenter.

- If the caller didn't enter one of the recognized code, we say goodbye and then hang up.

From this, it should be evident that Twilio's conferencing is really quite powerful, especially when you use the various customizable options to deal with things such as recordings, moderation, and the waiting experience.

 Twilio conferences only work with a maximum of 40 participants. If you need more callers than this, you'll need to stick with a traditional solution for the time being!

<Queue>

This final noun for <Dial> allows us to pull a call out of a queue to which we've added a call (that is, caller) with the <Enqueue> verb.

As with many of the previous nouns, we can specify a url attribute, pointing to a TwiML that will be played to the queued caller before they're put through to the person being dialed in.

Let's try it for ourselves:

```
<?xml version="1.0" encoding="UTF-8"?>
<Response>
  <Dial>
    <Queue url="alert.php">Support</Queue>
  </Dial>
</Response>
```

When this TwiML is executed, the caller will be connected to the next caller in the *support* queue after the person waiting in the queue has gone through the TwiML in alert.php.

Let's create an example alert.php file now, where we'll tell the person that their call will be recorded:

```
<?xml version="1.0" encoding="UTF-8"?>
<Response>
  <Say>Thank you for waiting - you're about to be connected to one
  of our support team members. All calls are recorded.</Say>
</Response>
```

<Hangup>

The `<Hangup>` verb ends a call. It's just used on its own as a self-closing tag with no nouns or attributes. In the next example, we say goodbye and then hang up:

```
<?xml version="1.0" encoding="UTF-8"?>
<Response>
  <Say>Goodbye.</Say>
  <Hangup />
</Response>
```

<Redirect>

The `<Redirect>` verb moves from executing the current TwiML to a different file on a different URL immediately, ignoring the rest of the TwiML in the current file.

Inside the `<Redirect>` verb, we provide the absolute URL or relative path of the TwiML file to be executed. We can also set the `method` attribute to `GET`; it defaults to `POST`:

```
<?xml version="1.0" encoding="UTF-8"?>
<Response>
  <Redirect method="GET">../other_twiml.php</Redirect>
</Response>
```

 The `<Redirect>` verb is not only applicable for phone calls. It is the only verb (except `<Message>` verb) that can be used for phone calls and incoming messages.

Nothing can be nested within the the `<Redirect>` verb, and any verbs after it are ignored as the redirect takes place right away.

<Reject>

The `<Reject>` verb, if placed as the *very first verb* in an incoming call, will prevent the call from being answered and will incur no cost whatsoever.

If placed elsewhere in the call, the call will hang up but we will still be charged up to that point.

The caller will hear an engaged or busy tone that we can customize through the `reason` attribute. We set the reason to `rejected` in order to play an engaged tone (which is the default) or set it to `busy` for a busy tone.

We can use this if we want to screen out certain types of calls. For example, imagine a situation where we're being spammed by a particular number:

```
<?xml version="1.0" encoding="UTF-8"?>
<Response>
  <?php if ($_POST['From'] == "+447969123456") { ?>
    <Reject reason="busy" />
  <?php } else { ?>
    <Redirect method="GET">../other_twiml.php</Redirect>
  <?php } ?>
</Response>
```

Best practices for working with TwiML

We'll discuss some some helpful tips that can be kept in mind when you're working with TwiML to make your application better organized, more easily testable, and more maintainable.

Test locally using ngrok

When you're working with and building a Twilio application, you'll need to test it frequently by making and receiving real calls on the platform, which requires Twilio to be able to access your local web server.

This is often a challenge with the perils of dynamic IP addresses and port forwarding. Fortunately, there's a great free tool called **ngrok** (`https://ngrok.com`), which will help you get around this problem.

It'll give you a special URL (for example, `http://123abc.ngrok.com`), which Twilio can use to reach your application. So, you can enter this on your numbers in your Dashboard in order to receive inbound calls and SMS messages.

ngrok is simple to use, but you'll need to be at least a little comfortable with the command line:

1. To get started, download the app for your platform from `http://ngrok.com`. It's currently available on Mac OS X, Windows, and Linux.

2. Start your web server. It can be running on port 80, which is the default HTTP port, but many web servers run on non-standard ports such as 8080 or 3000; both are supported.

3. Unzip `ngrok`, and then copy it to a location from where it is easily accessible. Ideally, it would be in your shell path, but to start with, you could keep it in your `Downloads` directory or somewhere else which is easy to access.

The next steps will differ somewhat, depending on whether you're on Windows or another platform.

Windows

1. Open a command prompt from the **Start** menu, and then use `cd` to navigate to the folder where ngrok is stored; see http://www.wikihow.com/Change-Directories-in-Command-Prompt if you're not sure how to do this.

2. Once you're there, run `ngrok` followed by the port your web server is running on (for example, `ngrok 80` if your server runs on port 80), and then hit Return.

Mac OS X and Linux (and others!)

Open a terminal and use `cd` to find the directory where the ngrok executable is stored. For help with navigating, see http://www.linfo.org/cd.html.

Once you're there, run `./ngrok`, followed by the port your web server is listening on, for instance, `./ngrok 3000` if your web server works on port 3000.

Once you've run ngrok, you'll see a screen that looks a little like this:

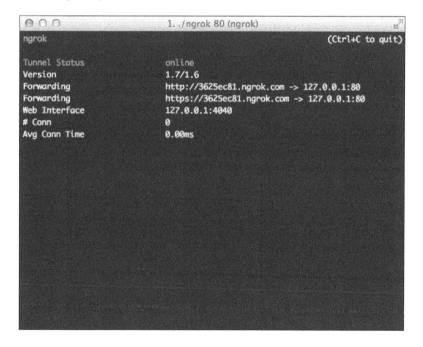

Just copy the second **Forwarding** URL — the one with HTTPS for additional security and you can use it to build a URL to enter in your Twilio dashboard.

For example, if my TwiML was located at `/voicemail/record.xml`, I'd enter the `https://3625ec81.ngrok.com/voicemail/record.xml` URL on Twilio in the previous ngrok session. You'll need to keep your `ngrok` session running for Twilio to be able to access your application, but once you're done, just hit *Ctrl + C*.

Make your application resilient with a fallback URL

The very nature of hosting an application is that despite your best intentions and efforts, your TwiML will be unavailable from time to time. This might be due to a bug or an electrical outage with your hosting provider.

With something as critical as a phone service, you want to be sure that when this happens, those using your service will see *at worst* a graceful degradation of the service they receive.

By default, in case of an error, Twilio will speak in its (somewhat robotic) text-to-speech voice:

> *"An application error has occurred. Goodbye."*

However, we want to provide a better experience than this. For example, in the case of a customer support phone system that will usually have complex menus and queuing, we might want to redirect the call to our switchboard if there was downtime. Twilio's **fallback URL** functionality makes this possible.

A fallback URL will be used by Twilio to fetch TwiML for an inbound call or SMS (and potentially, outbound calls too) if your usual server is unavailable or returns an error. Here, you'd store some default TwiML for use in a worst-case scenario. In the previous example, we might use something like this:

```xml
<?xml version="1.0" encoding="UTF-8"?>
<Response>
  <Say>Please wait while we connect you to our switchboard.</Say>
  <Dial>
    <Number>+441290211000</Number>
  </Dial>
</Response>
```

We can set up monitoring using Twilio's App Monitor Triggers so that we're informed as soon as our servers start experiencing problems. See *Chapter 7, Testing, Debugging, and deploying Twilio Apps,* for details.

It makes sense to make the fallback TwiML as simple as possible in order to avoid potential points of failure when our application is experiencing problems.

 Naturally, it's of integral importance that you host your fallback TwiML somewhere separate from your main application. I'd recommend *Amazon S3* (`http://aws.amazon.com/s3/`) as a particularly strong bet from an availability point of view.

We can set a fallback URL from the same **Numbers** page as where we set up our usual Voice and Messaging URLs. To do this, simply click on the **Optional Voice Settings** or **Optional Messaging Settings** button as appropriate, and then enter the location of your TwiML in the **Fallback URL** field. Finally, click on **Save**.

Fallback URL ⓘ	https://s3.amazonaws.com/twilio-best-practices/fallback.xml	HTTP GET ▾

Use Twilio's applications to manage your TwiML URLs

At the beginning of this chapter, we set up an inbound phone number by editing that number and setting a URL for Twilio to webhook whenever there's an inbound phone call or message.

This is all well and good, but it makes life much harder if we ever want to conduct maintenance on our application. For example, what if you have hundreds of numbers using the same URL, but you then need to change it?

Twilio provides a great solution for this in the form of **TwiML apps**. The app functionality lets you predefine sets of URLs that you can then assign to different phone numbers.

To create an app, in your Twilio dashboard navigation bar, go to **Dev Tools** and then go to **TwiML Apps** in the subnavigation:

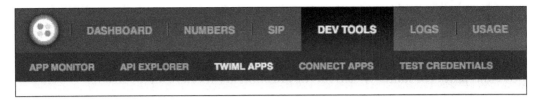

From there, click on the red **Create TwiML App** button. Specify a name, which is how you'll identify your app across Twilio's interface, and then you can set the various request URLs, just as you'd do for an individual phone number. Once you're done, hit **Save**:

 An app supports all of the same settings as an individual number, so it can even be used with a fallback URL for improved reliability.

Once you've created an app, you can easily assign it to phone numbers. To do this, head to the **Numbers** page, choose a number, and then click on **Configure with Application**. You'll then be able to choose the application you've just created from the list.

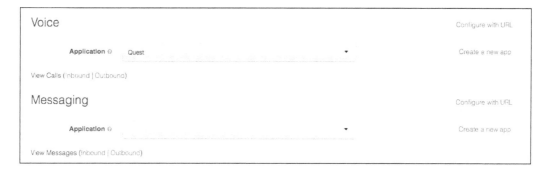

From now on, your phone number will stay updated as you make changes to the app. If, for example, you change the URL for an incoming SMS on your app, it'll propagate to each phone number it's attached to.

Summary

In this chapter, we learned what TwiML is and the three ways we'll use it: handling inbound calls, dealing with incoming messages, and telling Twilio what to do when we place outgoing calls.

We bought a phone number and then hooked it up to our TwiML. We also saw the data we get from Twilio in webhooks when there's an incoming call or message.

We respond to the webhooks with TwiML made up of verbs and nouns in order to decide what happens with the call, for instance, playing sound clips or sending SMS messages. For the various verbs, we saw helpful tips and tricks and learned best practices in order to work with TwiML more generally.

In the next chapter, we'll build on what we've learned and will start working with Twilio's REST API that, apart from allowing us to place outgoing calls and messages, will give us access to the wealth of data in our Twilio account.

2
Exploring the REST API

In this chapter, you'll learn the following topics:

- What the Twilio REST API is
- How the API works from a low-level perspective
- Working with Twilio's PHP API library
- Making RESTful requests directly using Postman
- How to make the most of the Calls and Messages APIs
- Turbo-charging your Twilio applications with Subaccounts, Phone Numbers, and Usage APIs

What is the Twilio REST API?

Twilio's REST API is the way in which you'll proactively interact with your Twilio account. This contrasts with TwiML, which is used to shape the flow of individual calls and incoming SMSes.

It programmatically gives you access to all of the data and features accessible from your Twilio dashboard, ranging from logs of previous calls to records of phone numbers you've purchased and is used to trigger outbound calls and SMS messages.

RESTful APIs are centered around data. Effectively, the API models various kinds of resources that Twilio holds, such as calls, phone numbers, or messages, and lets you perform **Create, Read, Update, Delete** (**CRUD**) operations on them.

If you're not familiar with REST APIs and how they work, IBM has a helpful primer at http://www.ibm.com/developerworks/library/ws-restful/.

Interacting with the API

Twilio's REST APIs are accessed over HTTP, that is to say, you make an HTTP request with the appropriate method, which is either GET, POST, PUT, or DELETE, and Twilio responds with data that represents the object you've created, read, updated, or deleted.

Fortunately, Twilio make our lives easier by providing **API libraries** in a range of languages. These are wrappers around the raw HTTP requests that Twilio understands, letting us interact with the API in a way that fits with the language we're working in.

At the time of writing, first-party API libraries (that is, libraries built by Twilio) are available in PHP, Ruby, Java, C#, Python, Node.js, and Apex (Salesforce's proprietary language). We'll want to use these when working with Twilio in our applications for the sake of simplicity and testability.

When getting started, it can be helpful to get a feel for working with the API by building the actual HTTP requests ourselves. There are a range of great tools for doing this, but in this chapter, we'll use a Chrome app called **Postman**.

Throughout the chapter, you'll see examples of using both the PHP client library (other libraries will be very similar) and raw HTTP requests built with Postman.

Authentication

When working with the Twilio API, we have to provide our **account SID** (a 34-character string starting with AC) and the **auth token** with every request. This is available at the top of your Dashboard when logged in, as seen here:

The Twilio API uses basic HTTP authentication, which means your account SID and auth token effectively function as a username and password.

When you enter a username and password on a website (including on Twilio's, for that matter), the password proves that we're a registered user and determines what data we're able to access and what we can do.

Twilio's API libraries deal with the authentication step for you, which means you can set the account SID and auth token when first initializing your application, and then they'll automatically be used for future requests.

Fetching existing data

First, let's look at using the REST API to query existing data that Twilio holds and then make changes to it.

Listing records

When we want to interact with data that already exists, we'll use an HTTP GET request.

For example, when we make a GET request to https://api.twilio.com/2010-04-01/Accounts/<our account SID>/Calls.json, Twilio responds with a list of Call resources, both inbound and outbound, that have passed through our account. This list is called the **index**.

If records were retrieved successfully, Twilio will respond with a 200 OK response.

As a default, Twilio responds with XML, but by appending .json to our request URL, we can request the more modern **JSON** format instead. This works across the Twilio API.

 I'd strongly recommend that you use JSON everywhere, as it is much simpler to understand and parse.

JSON stores data in simple key-value pairs (as opposed to XML's more complex data structures), which can be processed more efficiently and are more human-readable.

By including optional parameters with our HTTP request to the index, we can filter the data we get back.

A JSON list response looks something like this:

```
{
    ...
    "calls": [{
        "sid": "CA4c22bfc16f4b484d8b7cbe0f3c79bcc7",
        "date_created": "Tue, 12 Jun 2012 03:25:49 +0000",
        "date_updated": "Tue, 12 Jun 2012 03:27:05 +0000",
        "parent_call_sid": null,
        "account_sid": "AC387caf9bc67f4a52811b295ee0401949",
        "to": "+18085553279",
```

```
        "to_formatted": "(808) 555-3279",
        "from": "+17075559463",
        "from_formatted": "(707) 555-9463",
        "phone_number_sid": "PN907a2531e2d34c94b24b2794e73681de",
        "status": "completed",
        "start_time": "Tue, 12 Jun 2012 03:26:15 +0000",
        "end_time": "Tue, 12 Jun 2012 03:27:05 +0000",
        "duration": "50",
        "price": "-0.02000",
        "direction": "outbound-api",
        "answered_by": null,
        "api_version": "2010-04-01",
        "forwarded_from": null,
        "caller_name": null,
        "uri": "\/2010-04-01\/Accounts\/
AC387caf9bc67f4a52811b295ee0401949\/Calls\/
CA4c22bfc16f4b484d8b7cbe0f3c79bcc7.json",
        "subresource_uris": {
            "notifications": "\/2010-04-01\/
Accounts\/AC387caf9bc67f4a52811b295ee0401949\/Calls\/
CA4c22bfc16f4b484d8b7cbe0f3c79bcc7\/Notifications.json",
            "recordings": "\/2010-04-01\/Accounts\/
AC387caf9bc67f4a52811b295ee0401949\/Calls\/
CA4c22bfc16f4b484d8b7cbe0f3c79bcc7\/Recordings.json"
        }
    }, ... ]
}
```

Pagination

It's likely that listing records will return many results. For this reason, Twilio uses pagination, splitting indexes into multiple pages that require multiple HTTP requests.

By default, Twilio will load 50 records per page, but you can increase this to a maximum of 1,000 by setting the `PageSize` parameter.

In its responses, Twilio gives information on how to navigate between pages, primarily in the form of the `NextPageUrl` and `LastPageUrl` attributes. What you get back for a paginated response will be something like this:

```
{
    "page": 0,
    "num_pages": 3,
    "page_size": 50,
    "total": 147,
    "start": 0,
```

```
    "end": 49,
    "uri": "\/2010-04-01\/Accounts\/
AC228b97a5fe4138be081eaff3c44180f3\/Calls.json",
    "first_page_uri": "\/2010-04-01\/Accounts\/
AC228b97a5fe4138be081eaff3c44180f3\/Calls.json?Page=0&PageSize=50",
    "previous_page_uri": null,
    "next_page_uri": "\/2010-04-01\/Accounts\/
AC228b97a5fe4138be081eaff3c44180f3\/Calls.json?Page=1&PageSize=50&Afte
rSid=CA228399228abecca920de212121",
    "last_page_uri": "\/2010-04-01\/Accounts\/
AC228b97a5fe4138be081eaff3c44180f3\/Calls.json?Page=2&PageSize=50"
```

These URLs can be used to navigate between pages, and are for that matter the mechanism that Twilio's API libraries use to do this.

Fetching an individual record

In a similar way, we can also fetch individual records once we have their **SID** (a unique Twilio identifier tied to each record regardless of type). While we can obtain this from the index, we can also have it stored when we originally created the record.

For instance, we load an individual call record by making a GET request to the `https://api.twilio.com/2010-04-01/Accounts/<our account SID>/Calls/<call SID>.json` URL.

If all has gone as per the plan, the status code will be 200 OK, but a number of errors (for instance, 404 Not Found) might occur; see the *Handling errors* section later in this chapter for details.

Twilio responds with data that represents an individual call if it was found successfully. You'll get something like this example of a Message resource, which represents an MMS/SMS:

```
{
    "sid": "SM1f0e8ae6ade43cb3c0ce4525424e404f",
    "date_created": "Fri, 13 Aug 2010 01:16:24 +0000",
    "date_updated": "Fri, 13 Aug 2010 01:16:24 +0000",
    "date_sent": null,
    "account_sid": "AC228b97a5fe4138be081eaff3c44180f3",
    "to": "+15305431221",
    "from": "+15104564545",
    "body": "A Test Message",
    "status": "queued",
    "flags":["outbound"],
    "api_version": "2010-04-01",
```

```
    "price": null,
    "uri": "\/2010-04-01\/Accounts\/
AC228ba7a5fe4238be081ea6f3c44186f3\/SMS\/Messages\/
SM1f0e8ae6ade43cb3c0ce4525424e404f.json"
}
```

Creating new records

To create a new record, we'll make an HTTP POST request to Twilio's index for the type of resource we're looking to create, with the data for the new record in the body.

For instance, to send an SMS, following RESTful API semantics, we make a POST request to the Messages index at https://api.twilio.com/2010-04-01/ Accounts/<account SID>/Messages.json.

Here, we include the number the message should be sent from (the From attribute), the destination number (the To attribute), and the contents of the message (the Body attribute) we want to send in the **request body**.

If the record was created as expected, we receive a 201 Created response plus a representation of the Message resource we've just created. This will include its SID, which we can use to fetch the same record in the future.

What you'll get back will be exactly the same as if you had just fetched the individual resource. For an example, see the *Fetching an individual record* section earlier in this chapter.

Modifying existing records

To modify an existing record, we'll make an HTTP POST to the URL of the individual record we're working against.

For instance, to change a call currently in progress to use different TwiML, we make a POST request to https://api.twilio.com/2010-04-01/Accounts/<account SID>/Calls/<call SID>.json.

In the request body, we include the URL of the TwiML we'd like to use (the Url attribute) and optionally, the HTTP method to request this TwiML with (Method, which defaults to POST).

Twilio responds with a representation of the resource in its modified state, plus a status of 200 OK if the record was updated successfully. Again, see the *Fetching an individual record* section, for an example response.

Deleting an existing record

To delete an existing record, we'll make an HTTP DELETE request to the URL of the individual resource we want to delete.

For example, to delete a Recording resource, which represents a recording Twilio has created from a call, we make a DELETE request to https://api.twilio.com/2010-04-01/Accounts/<account SID>/Recordings/<recording SID>.json.

Twilio responds with a representation of the resource we've just deleted plus a status of 204 OK if the record was successfully deleted.

Handling errors

If all goes as per the plan, we'll receive a 2XX response (200, 201, or 204 depending on the operation you're trying to complete).

However, if something goes wrong, from the record requested not existing to the account SID and auth token being invalid, you'll get a different response code.

Here's a list of the response codes Twilio uses, plus what they mean:

Code	What it means?
200, 201 or 204	Everything went as expected; the resource was found, created, deleted, or updated as requested.
302	The resource you requested exists, but should be accessed at a different location (that is, the URL). The correct URL will be found in the Location response header.
400	The data you included in the request was invalid; see the response body (either XML or JSON) for specifics of the error (details in the next example).
401	The account SID and auth token you provided to authenticate with were invalid. Replace these with correct ones and try again.
404	The resource you requested wasn't found; check the URL you're using or the SID provided (which is more likely).
405	The object you're attempting to delete cannot be deleted (for example, a Call).

Code	What it means?
429	The Twilio API is rejecting your request because you've made too many other API calls recently/simultaneously. Try again later.
500	Twilio experienced an error of some kind; you've probably discovered a bug! Try again later.

If you receive an error response, Twilio will include details on the actual error that occurred in the response body.

This is particularly useful for `400 Bad Request` responses. This response is returned when you've provided data to update or create a record, but the data is invalid or incomplete.

In the body, you'll find further details on the specific issue that occurred (for example, what attribute was missing or invalid), including a link to tips on fixing the error.

The response you get will look like this (note that the `Code` and `MoreInfo` elements will only be included for `400` responses):

```
{
    "status": 400,
    "message": "No to number is specified",
    "code": 21201,
    "more_info": "http:\/\/www.twilio.com\/docs\/errors\/21201"
}
```

When working with one of Twilio's API libraries, generally speaking, an exception will be raised whenever the Twilio API responds with an error.

Getting started with the Twilio PHP library

When you use one of Twilio's API libraries instead of working directly with more low-level HTTP requests, you'll interact with Twilio using simpler code that abstracts away details such as forming URLs, authenticating, and catching errors.

Twilio offers libraries in most major languages, but we'll look at PHP in order to stay in sync with *Chapter 1, Working with TwiML*.

The principles will be similar if you're using another language, but the syntax and grammar will be different. To see Twilio in action in Ruby, Python, C#, Java, Node.js, and Apex, head to *Chapter 5, Twilio in your language*.

Downloading the PHP library

First, you'll need to download the library. There are two options for doing this, which are matched across most languages you might use.

Downloading the code manually

Twilio publishes the source code for its API libraries on **GitHub** (https://github.com). GitHub is the most popular platform for online sharing and collaborating on code and is based on the popular Git version control software, which itself is open source.

From each library's GitHub repository, you can download its code as a ZIP or TAR file for inclusion into your project. You'll find the **twilio-php** repository at https://github.com/twilio/twilio-php.

Once you're there, click on the **releases** link at the top of the page.

Next, click on the **Source code (zip)** button for the most recent version of the library. A ZIP file containing the current release will be downloaded, which you should unzip.

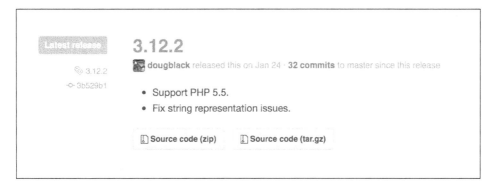

Now that you've got a copy of the library, you'll need to copy it into your project. Copy the entire contents of the ZIP file somewhere into your directory structure. Depending on how you organize your code and/or the framework you're using, a location such as `includes/twilio-php` will most likely be sensible.

You'll then include the library, replacing /path/to with the path to your twilio-php directory, of course:

```
require '/path/to/twilio-php/Services/Twilio.php';
```

> You'll most likely require Twilio.php in various places across your projects, so rather than doing this repeatedly in every file, you should add a bootstrapping file (for example, twilio.inc.php) to load the library and then configure it.

This process will be similar in any language you're working in.

Using a package manager

Downloading code manually is not a particularly good way to manage external dependencies. It means messy require calls and a tough time every time you want to update a library.

The modern solution to this problem across programming languages is to use a package manager. It manages your dependencies for you, typically making it easy to autoload them and making updating an external library as simple as a command-line command.

In PHP, the de facto standard in dependency management is **Composer** (https://getcomposer.org), but other languages have their own standards, for instance, NPM in Node.js or Bundler in the Ruby world.

If you're using a modern framework for your PHP projects, such as Laravel (http://laravel.com—I highly recommend it), you're probably already familiar with Composer, but if you're not, I'd recommend the tool's own *getting started* guide at https://getcomposer.org/doc/00-intro.md.

> Pay special attention to the *Autoload* section at the bottom of the guide. This particularly powerful feature of Composer will let you automatically load all of your dependencies with just one require call.

Once you're set up with Composer, just run a command in your shell to add the Twilio library to your project:

```
composer require twilio/sdk dev-master
```

The library will be downloaded and added to your `vendor/autoload.php` file and will be ready to go with automatic loading for use in your code.

Getting started

Once you've got the library installed and everything is accounted for, it's simple to use it as and when it's needed.

All you'll need to do is instantiate the `Services_Twilio` object using your account SID and auth token. The library will need these in order to automatically authenticate all of the requests you make.

Setting up the client looks like this:

```php
<?php
// First, require the library's Twilio.php file or bring
in your Composer autoload.php

// ...
$sid = "ACXXXXXX"; // Your Account SID from www.twilio.com/user/
account
$token = "YYYYYY"; // Your Auth Token from www.twilio.com/user/account
$client = new Services_Twilio($sid, $token);
?>
```

Now, when you want to interact with Twilio, you'll call various methods on the `$client` object you've just created, such as this example of sending an SMS:

```php
<?php
// …
$message = $client->account->messages->sendMessage(
  "+441290211999",
  "+441290211998",
  "This is a test message from the first number to the second one."
);
?>
```

As you'll see, using the library makes a big difference to your coding experience. Rather than manually making a `POST` request to `https://api.twilio.com/2010-04-01/Accounts/{our account SID}/Messages` and forming the correct parameters and headers, we can call a very normal-looking PHP method.

Next, we're going to see how to set up Postman to make manual API requests that are perfect for experimenting with the Twilio API and are also useful for other APIs you might play with.

Getting started with Postman

Postman is a great tool to play with APIs such as Twilio's and even to test your own. It comes in the form of a Chrome application, and lets you build, create, and save HTTP requests, keeping track of what you sent and the response you got back.

To get started, you'll need to make sure that you have Google Chrome installed (`http://chrome.google.com`), and then you can download Postman from Chrome's Web Store at `https://chrome.google.com/webstore/detail/postman-rest-client-packa/fhbjgbiflinjbdggehcddcbncdddomop?hl=en`.

Once installed, you'll be able to use Postman from Chrome's **Apps** screen. It'll also be installed as a standalone application that will be available from your `Applications` folder and Spotlight on Mac OS X, or from the Start menu on Windows.

Making your first request with Postman

Now that we have Postman installed, let's set it up to make requests to Twilio. We'll go through its interface and set everything up as we go.

First, we'll set up our authentication details. Click on **Basic Auth** at the top, and then fill in your account SID and auth token into the **Username** and **Password** fields, respectively:

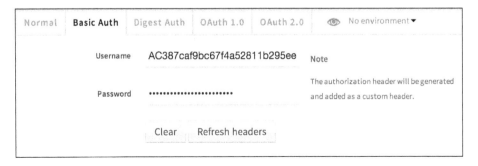

To the right of the **Basic Auth** option, you'll see the environment drop-down. You can use this to save your authentication details and other parts of your Twilio request.

Just below the dropdown is where you'll enter the URL for your request. To start, let's just do something really simple and grab a list of our account's phone numbers.

To do that, enter the URL for the `IncomingPhoneNumber` resource's index, which is `https://api.twilio.com/2010-04-01/Accounts/<your account SID>/IncomingPhoneNumbers.json` (replace `<your account SID>` with the account SID we used as our username).

Check whether the dropdown to the right is set to **GET**, and then hit the **Send** button.

 In most Twilio API URLs, you'll need to include your account SID. This is the same as the username you're using for basic authentication, so just copy it across.

Below the dropdown, all being well, you'll see some beautifully formatted JSON. This is the response Postman has received from Twilio:

```
Pretty   Raw   Preview            Q   ≡⊦      JSON ▾

{
    first_page_uri: /2010-04-01/Accounts/AC31e4ac3e57344b84a7f35ebcbbec0a91/IncomingPhoneNumbers.json?Page=0&PageSize=50,
    end: 6,
    previous_page_uri: null,
  - incoming_phone_numbers: [
      - {
            sid: "PNff98f0980aa3fae76c2fa4423ae764b2",
            account_sid: "AC31e4ac3e57344b84a7f35ebcbbec0a91",
            friendly_name: "(415) 802-0556",
            phone_number: "+14158020556",
            voice_url: https://demo.twilio.com/welcome/voice/,
            voice_method: "POST",
            voice_fallback_url: "",
            voice_fallback_method: "POST",
```

Postman also gives us a range of other helpful information to make our lives easier.

Above and to the right of the response, we'll see the HTTP status code that came back with the response, plus the time it took for the request to be executed.

We can also click to see the response headers from Twilio. This can often be useful in order to understand what's going on, and some parts of the Twilio (for example, its SIP functionality) make use of these headers in significant ways.

Getting the most out of Postman

We've seen the basics of Postman and made our first request. Let's find out a little more so that we can make full use of it.

Sending parameters

Lots of Twilio requests require parameters, whether it is to filter lists with a GET request or to specify details in a POST request when placing a call.

To provide parameters, choose your request method (either **GET, POST,** or **DELETE**) from the dropdown, and then click on the **URL params** button to the right.

A new set of fields where you can specify key-value pairs will appear. Let's try to filter our list of incoming phone numbers from before.

Take the same URL as the one used previously, but add a parameter entry with a PhoneNumber key to filter for only UK phone numbers. Just add an entry with PhoneNumber as the key and **44*** as the value, and then click on **Send**.

We'll get a new set of filtered results back. Filters available for many of the API resources will be covered later in this chapter, but full lists are available at Twilio's REST API documentation at `https://www.twilio.com/docs/api/rest`.

If you're creating or updating a resource using a `POST` request (for instance, placing a call or buying a phone number), you'll specify parameters in exactly the same way.

Using History and Collections

Postman provides two really great features that help you keep track of previous requests: **History** and **Collections**.

Whenever you make a request, Postman will keep a record of it in the left-hand sidebar. Just click on the request in the list, and all of its parameters and settings will be prepopulated on the right-hand side, ready for you to hit **Send** in order to run it once again.

If you want something a bit more permanent, and/or you want to organize and categorize your requests, you can use **Collections**.

Once you've set up a useful request and it's working, click on the **Add to collection** button to the right of the **Send** button that we've already been using.

Let's try to set up a collection for the request we were working with in the *Making your first request with Postman* section.

First, name your collection. This is a group that will help you organize and find your saved requests later. Next, provide a name for this particular request, and then — if you like — write a fuller description for it. Once you're done, click on **Add to collection** at the bottom, as seen here.

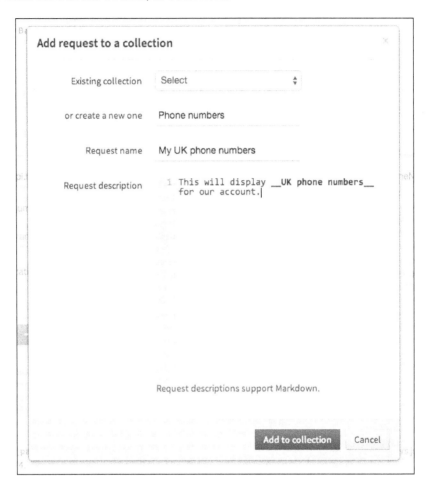

To view our collections, click on **Collections**, which is above the **History** tab we were looking at previously. You'll see your new entry under the collection you specified:

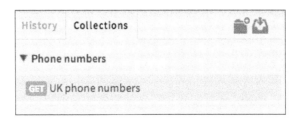

As with the records in your history, click on the entry and you'll see all of the settings populated on the right-hand side, plus the title and description we specified earlier:

Mastering call-related APIs

Now that we know in more abstract terms how the Twilio API works and have had an introduction to the PHP library and Postman, let's try our hand at playing with the API for real, starting with the Call resource.

All of our examples will include the URL and parameters you can use with Postman, plus a code sample for the PHP library.

Making a call

To make a call, we'll need to make a POST request to `https://api.twilio.com/2010-04-01/Accounts/<your account SID>/Calls.json` with the following parameters:

Parameter	Explanation
From	This refers to the phone number that will be used as the caller ID for this call (this must be one of your Twilio numbers or another one you own and have verified with Twilio).
To	This refers to the phone number you need to dial.
Url	This refers to a URL that serves TwiML, which should be used to handle this call. Either this or ApplicationSid must be specified.
ApplicationSid	This refers to the SID of an application that specifies a TwiML URL that can be used for your call; see the *Use Twilio's applications to manage your TwiML URLs* section in *Chapter 1, Working with TwiML* for details. Either this or Url must be specified.

On top of these, there are some optional parameters you can specify, such as `Method` (the HTTP method with which Twilio should request the TwiML) and `SendDigits` (touch-tone digits that are sent as soon as the call is answered).

See Twilio's documentation at `https://www.twilio.com/docs/api/rest/making-calls#post-parameters-optional` for a full list of options.

In order to use a phone number that you haven't bought through Twilio as your caller ID, you'll need to verify it. To do this, Twilio will call the number and have you enter a verification code. Doing this takes just a minute or so.

Head to `https://www.twilio.com/user/account/phone-numbers/verified` and click on **Verify a number**, or see the *Phone Numbers* section to learn how to do this programmatically.

To make the preceding request in Postman, simply copy the URL, filling in your account SID, and then transpose the relevant parameters into the **URL params** fields before clicking on **Send**.

Twilio responds with JSON, representing the call we've just placed.

To do the same thing in PHP, once you've got your Twilio Client instance set up, simply run some code like this:

```php
<?php
$call = $client->account->calls->create(
  "+441290211998", // Number to call from
  "+441290211999", // Number to call to
  "http://assets.twiliobestpractices.com/sample.xml"
);
// The call we've just created - grabbed from the API response - is
saved to $call and all its attributes are accessible
echo $call->sid;
?>
```

Following the standard convention, the Twilio API responds with a JSON representation of the call, which the PHP automatically marshals into an easy-to-access object. This is why we can easily call `$call->sid` or `$message->status` to fetch details about the call we've just placed.

For a full list of the parameters available for different methods in the PHP library, such as the `create` method we saw previously, see the library documentation at `https://twilio-php.readthedocs.org/en/latest/api/rest.html`.

Once we've placed a call, we'll find it in the logs for our account at
`https://www.twilio.com/user/account/log/calls`.

Working with an existing call

We've placed a call, so we'll now have its SID (which we echoed in the last example).
With this, we can fetch the Call using the API in order to find out more details about
it, and particularly to check up on its status. This will work with the SID for any call,
whether it is outbound (that is, initiated by us) or inbound.

To do this, we'll make a `GET` request to `https://api.twilio.com/2010-04-01/`
`Accounts/<your account SID>/Calls/<call SID>.json`.

There's no need for any parameters, so if we're authenticated and have provided a
valid SID, we'll get JSON, representing our call.

Similarly, in the PHP library, we'd load a call record like this:

```
$call = $client->account->calls->get("my call SID");
echo $call->status; // Display the call's current status
```

Once we've loaded the call, there's lots of information we can learn about, from when
it finished to how much it cost in Twilio credit. See `https://www.twilio.com/`
`docs/api/rest/call#instance` for all the attributes.

If the call is still in progress — that is, if its `status` attribute is `in-progress` — we
can redirect it to use different TwiML via the API. For instance, I do this in one
application to connect a call once a customer service agent is ready to pick it up.

To do this, make a `POST` request to `https://api.twilio.com/2010-04-01/`
`Accounts/<your account SID>/Calls/<call SID>.json`, including a `Url`
parameter (and an optional `Method` parameter), specifying the URL of the TwiML
you'd like to use.

In the PHP library, load the Call record as you did previously, and then do
the following:

```
$call->update(array(
  "Url" => "http://timrogers.uk/path/to/twiml",
  "Method" => "POST"
));
```

If you're just checking the status of a call, you shouldn't generally be fetching it with the API, but should be using Twilio's event-driven status callbacks, where Twilio will notify you once a call finishes. See `https://www.twilio.com/docs/api/twiml/twilio_request#asynchronous` for details, although we'll cover this in more detail in *Chapter 4, Twilio in the Real World*.

Listing previous calls

We can see and track all our calls from our Twilio dashboard, but we can also use the API! Simply make a GET request to `https://api.twilio.com/2010-04-01/Accounts/<your account SID>/Calls.json`—no parameters needed—and we'll get a response with a list of both inbound and outbound calls on our account.

The only complication here comes when we have more than 50 records, as Twilio only shows 50 records at a time. We'll need to get to grips with the API's pagination.

When working with Postman, scroll to the bottom of your response and you'll see the `next_page_uri` parameter if there are more records to fetch. Copy this into the URL field, and you'll get the next page, and so on.

In the PHP library, fetching our call list looks like this:

```
$calls = $client->account->calls;
```

From this, we'll get a `Services_Twilio_Rest_Calls` object from the API library, which behaves like an array that we can loop through.

However, this doesn't deal with the pagination issue, and we can't directly access `next_page_uri` as we might in Postman.

Fortunately, the library provides a useful `getIterator` method for index methods across the PHP library. This deals with the pagination for you. Using it can be as simple as this:

```
// The first parameter to getIterator, "0", refers to the page of
// results to start from
foreach ($client->account->calls->getIterator(0) as $call) {
  echo $call->sid;
}
```

Using this method, the library will deal with iterating through the pages for you, which means you can ignore this complication entirely.

With `getIterator`, as well as the page you want to start with, you can provide two other parameters: the number of records to load per page (which defaults to 50) and a set of filters to filter the results, which is particularly useful.

To see how these options work, see the library's documentation at `https://twilio-php.readthedocs.org/en/latest/api/rest.html?highlight=page#Services_Twilio_ListResource::getIterator`.

Mastering messaging APIs

We've now seen how easy it is to make phone calls and work with them. Similar concepts work in order to send SMS and MMS messages, so we'll look at those next.

Sending your first SMS

To send an SMS, make a `POST` request to `https://api.twilio.com/2010-04-01/Accounts/<your account SID>/Messages.json` with the following parameters:

Parameter	Explanation
From	The phone number to be used as the caller ID for this message (it must be one of your Twilio numbers or another one you own and have verified with Twilio)
To	The phone number to send the message to
Body	The text you'd like to send in the SMS

As you might be aware, a single SMS can contain a maximum of 160 characters. If you include more than this in the `Body` parameter, Twilio will automatically segment and **concatenate** your messages so that they arrive on the recipient's device as one (although you'll have to pay for the number of messages actually sent) as long as this is supported by their carrier.

As is the case with most of the Twilio APIs, there are a number of optional parameters you can use if you wish. For instance, `StatusCallback`, which allows you to get updates on the delivery of your message. For full details, see `https://www.twilio.com/docs/api/rest/sending-messages#post-DONEparameters-optional`.

Using the PHP library, sending a message is super simple:

```
$message = $client->account->messages->sendMessage
("+441290211998", "+441290211999", "This is a message from the first
number, to the second, with this in the body.");
echo $message->sid . " is " . $message->status;
```

We'll find the message we've just sent in the logs of our Twilio account at
`https://www.twilio.com/user/account/log/messages`.

Sending images using MMS

A relatively recent feature in the Twilio API, which first launched in September,
2013, is the ability to send MMS messages which includes images rather than simple
plain text. We've already seen this with the `<Message>` verb in *Chapter 1, Working
with TwiML*.

 Sending MMS messages isn't yet available in all of the markets
where Twilio offers phone numbers, so check `https://www.`
`twilio.com/help/faq/phone-numbers/how-do-i-check-`
`if-my-twilio-number-can-send-picture-messages`
before you give it a go.

Sending an MMS is pretty much as easy as sending an SMS.

Using Postman, simply add a `MediaUrl` parameter, which links to the GIF, PNG,
or JPEG image you'd like to send, making a POST request to `https://api.twilio.`
`com/2010-04-01/Accounts/<your account SID>/Messages.json`, just like you
did to send an SMS.

In the PHP library, simply add a fourth parameter with the image's URL to the
`sendMessage` method as follows:

```
$message = $client->account->messages->sendMessage("+441290211998",
"+441290211999", "Here's your boarding pass - make sure you keep
it safe on your device!", "http://assets.twiliobestpractices.com/
boarding-pass.png");
echo $message->sid;
```

You can leave out the `Body` parameter, thereby sending just the picture, or you can
include both which will send your image plus some text.

By passing an array to the fourth argument of the `sendMessage` method, we can send
more than one image.

Fetching an existing message

We've sent a couple of messages earlier—an SMS and an MMS—so we can now grab these via the API. To do this, we'll simply make a GET request to `https://api.twilio.com/2010-04-01/Accounts/<your account SID>/Messages/<SID>.json`, and Twilio will respond with JSON, representing our Message resource.

 Fetching isn't limited to only the outbound messages we've sent. If we have the SID of a message we've received, which is taken from the `MessageSid` parameter when the message was originally pinged to us, we can look that up as well.

In the PHP library, we can fetch a message as follows, getting back an object that represents the message:

```
$message = $client->account->messages->get("my message SID");
echo $message->status; // Display the message's current status
echo "This message cost " . $message->price . " to send.";
```

The API provides plenty of additional details about the message, from the number of segments it was split into to the number the message was sent to. See `https://www.twilio.com/docs/api/rest/#instance` for all of the attributes.

The `status` attribute is particularly useful because it allows us to work out whether the message has been received by the intended recipient and if not, why it wasn't received. In particular, if the status is undelivered, we can refer to `errorCode` and `errorMessage` to see why the message wasn't delivered successfully.

Listing previous messages

To list our previous incoming and outgoing messages, we simply make a GET request to `https://api.twilio.com/2010-04-01/Accounts/<your account SID>/Messages.json`.

We'll get a list back of messages in the JSON form.

In the PHP library, grabbing our previous messages looks like this:

```
$messages = $client->account->messages;
```

Let's try to loop through our messages and make use of the filtering options on the PHP library's `getIterator` method in order to find texts sent and received during September, 2014:

```
foreach ($client->account->messages->getIterator(0, 50,
array("DateCreated>=" => "2014-09-01", "DateCreated<" => "2014-10-01")
as $message) {
  echo $message->sid . "was sent or received in September.<br />";
}
```

> The `getIterator` method allows us to specify filters, combining the automatic handling of multiple pages with the ability to control the records we get back. This can be used across the PHP library.

Working with phone numbers, accounts, and usage

Now that we've looked at the core resources of the REST API—the Call and the Message—let's get to grips with some other interesting and useful parts.

Phone numbers

In the API, phone numbers are encapsulated into a number of different types of resources: the **AvailablePhoneNumber**, the **IncomingPhoneNumber**, the **OutgoingCallerId**, and the **ShortCode**.

Here, we're going to focus on dealing with numbers we'll actually buy through Twilio with AvailablePhoneNumber and IncomingPhoneNumber, but we'll briefly cover the remaining two.

We can purchase phone numbers via our Twilio **Dashboard**, but there are plenty of use cases where we might want to do this via the API, for instance, where we want to offer on-demand phone numbers to our users.

To get started, let's check what phone numbers are available for purchase by working with the AvailablePhoneNumber API.

To start, let's find an SMS-capable number in California, containing `123`. To do this directly with the REST API using Postman, we make a `GET` request to `https://api.twilio.com/2010-04-01/Accounts/<your account SID>/AvailablePhoneNumbers/US.json`.

This part of the API is a little strange in that we specify the country code for the number in the URL. Here, US stands for the United States.

For a full list of country codes and to better understand the options available, see `https://www.twilio.com/docs/api/rest/available-phone-numbers#countries`.

We can filter our request to SMS-capable numbers in California that contain the digits `123` by adding some parameters:

Key	Explanation	Value
InRegion	This refers to the region (in this case, the state) where we're looking for a number	CA
Contains	This refers to a pattern that can be looked for in the number (which might include asterisks as wildcard characters)	123
SmsEnabled	This determines whether the number should be SMS capable	true

The API supports a number of other parameters including `AreaCode`, `MmsEnabled`, and `VoiceEnabled`. We won't go into details about these parameters here, but they are relatively self-explanatory!

Let's try doing what we just saw using the PHP library:

```php
$phone_numbers = $client->account->available_phone_numbers-
>getList('US', 'Local', array('InRegion' => 'CA', 'Contains' => '123',
'SmsEnabled' => 'true'));

foreach ($phone_numbers->available_phone_numbers as $number) {
  echo $number->phone_number;
}
```

Whichever way we do this, via the PHP library or by making requests directly, we'll get back a list of available phone numbers (assuming that there's at least one that matches our criteria).

Let's go ahead and buy this phone number by moving to the IncomingPhoneNumber resource.

To buy a phone number, we'll make a POST request to the IncomingPhoneNumber resource's index at `https://api.twilio.com/2010-04-01/Accounts/<your account SID>/IncomingPhoneNumbers.json`, supplying a `PhoneNumber` parameter that contains the phone number to be purchased.

Using the PHP library, this is as simple as the following code:

```
$phoneNumber = $client->account->incoming_phone_numbers->create(array(
  "PhoneNumber" => "+14121234567"
));

echo $phoneNumber->sid;
```

You can even set key attributes of the phone number from its `FriendlyName` to the URLs that will be requested for TwiML when there's an incoming call or SMS (`VoiceUrl` and `SmsUrl`) at the point of purchase. Simply include these in the POST request or in the array passed into the `create` method provided by the PHP library.

A full list of these options is available at `https://www.twilio.com/docs/api/rest/incoming-phone-numbers#list-post-optional-parameters`.

Now that we've set up our phone number, we can easily load it via its SID and make changes to its attributes. We'll also be able to see it from the Twilio website at `https://www.twilio.com/user/account/phone-numbers/incoming` and make changes to it there.

To load an existing IncomingPhoneNumber, simply make a GET request to `https://api.twilio.com/2010-04-01/Accounts/<your account SID>/IncomingPhoneNumbers/<Phone number SID>.json` or load it with the PHP library by calling the following:

```
$phoneNumber = $client->account->incoming_phone_numbers->get("<sid>");
```

To change its attributes, simply make a POST request to the preceding URL, specifying the attributes to be updated. Another option when, working in PHP is to, call the `update` method on the previously returned `$phoneNumber` object with an array passed in:

```
$phoneNumber->update(array("FriendlyName" => "California number"));
```

Outgoing caller IDs

OutgoingCallerId resources represent phone numbers that you can use as the caller ID when making outgoing calls.

In order to use a number in this way, Twilio requires you to verify that you own it. To do this, they'll call you and ask you to enter a provided code.

This process can be triggered from the Twilio website but can also be started programmatically. This is likely to be helpful where you want your users to be able to set up their own caller IDs on demand.

To verify a number, make a `POST` request to `https://api.twilio.com/2010-04-01/Accounts/<your account SID>/OutgoingCallerIds.json`, including a `PhoneNumber` parameter.

In the PHP library, begin the process as follows:

```
$client->account->outgoing_caller_ids->create("<number to verify, in
international format>");
```

There are a couple of additional options available here, such as `CallDelay` which lets you ask Twilio to wait for a given number of seconds before calling the number and `StatusCallback`, which will let you receive a notification as to whether the number is successfully verified. See `https://www.twilio.com/docs/api/rest/outgoing-caller-ids#list-post-optional-parameters` for a full list.

If you're using PHP, you can pass an array of additional options as the parameter following the number itself.

In response, there'll be a `ValidationCode` attribute. This is the number you'll need to provide to users for them to enter into their phone when Twilio calls. Once they've entered it correctly, the number will be available as one of your caller IDs.

Once set up, our newly verified caller ID will appear at `https://www.twilio.com/user/account/phone-numbers/verified`.

Short codes

Short codes are special phone numbers, usually with a length of 5 or 6 digits, that are used for SMSes. They're easier for consumers to remember and dial. They're also required by Twilio if you're going to be sending a significant volume of SMSes.

These numbers cannot be bought through the API like normal ones and are of little interest, so I won't cover them in as much detail as I have covered other resources.

The API allows you to, as with normal numbers, view and update your short codes, and set details such as their friendly name and TwiML URLs.

Accounts

Working with **accounts** (or more to the point, **subaccounts**), much like the applications feature we looked at in the previous chapter, makes it easier to manage your use of Twilio.

As you have seen across the API so far, all URLs contain the SID of an application. When you create your login with Twilio, a default (or master) account is set up automatically. This is the one that you're effectively using as the username for the API, but it's possible to set up additional child accounts.

When you set up a child account, you'll be able to access it using your existing API credentials, but it can have its own phone numbers, usage records, and other resources while still being billed to you.

To see how this can be useful, imagine you're running a SaaS application that makes use of Twilio by providing a service to your customers. For instance, imagine that you're offering a call-center-as-a-service like the one we'll build in *Chapter 4, Twilio in the Real World*.

Your customers will each have their own phone numbers and you might want to segregate their usage records to bill them more easily. By setting up a subaccount, you can do all of this and more automatically.

Creating a subaccount

Imagine that a new customer is onboarding with our SaaS. We're going to need to buy them some Twilio numbers. Let's first create a subaccount using the API.

If you're using the REST API directly, you'll be making a `POST` request to `https://api.twilio.com/2010-04-01/Accounts.json` with a single parameter: `FriendlyName`. This will be used to identify the account.

This parameter isn't actually required, but it's good practice to provide it. If you don't specify one, Twilio will automatically generate a name for you with the date and time.

 For `FriendlyName`, you'll probably want to use the primary key of the new customer's record in your database or a Twilio identifier you generate specially.

In the PHP library, it is equally simple to create a subaccount:

```
$account = $client->accounts->create(array(
  "FriendlyName" => "Customer 123"
));
echo $account->sid;
```

We'll want to make sure we store the returned SID somewhere, as this is what we'll use to work with this account later. We'll also see our new subaccount and will be able to interact with it from the **Subaccounts** page on our Twilio dashboard at `https://www.twilio.com/user/account/subaccounts`.

Managing an account's resources

Now that we've created our subaccount, we'll want to use it when working with the API, for example, buying phone numbers and sending messages.

All we need in order to do this is its SID, and we can continue to authenticate our subaccount using our master account's SID and auth token.

If you're making REST API requests directly, this part is remarkably easy. You might have noticed that in all of our URLs (for example, `https://api.twilio.com/2010-04-01/Accounts/<account SID>/Messages.json`), there's been a placeholder for an account SID. Simply use the SID of our subaccount there and follow the instructions given earlier in the chapter.

Things are a little harder in the PHP library, but they still follow a simple convention that makes working with our subaccounts easy. Previously, we loaded our account's Messages like this:

```
$messages = $client->account->messages;
```

Now, we'd do something like this, referring directly to the subaccount we want to work with. By default, the PHP library infers the account SID to be used from the authentication details we provided when instantiating it:

```
$messages = $client->accounts->get("<subaccount SID>")->messages;
```

We'll follow this same convention everywhere to attribute what we're doing to our subaccount rather than the master one.

Suspending or closing a subaccount

Imagine that one of our customers has left our service or has failed to pay their invoice for a few months.

In this situation, we'd like to restrict their account, taking away access to their phone numbers and preventing them from incurring any more costs. This is very simple when we're using subaccounts to manage our use of Twilio.

Suspending an account

Suspending an account will stop it from being used to make and receive calls and messages, but this will keep its phone numbers going at the usual cost.

This might be useful in a situation where a customer has failed to pay, but you don't want to release the phone number(s) into the ether in case the customer comes back.

To suspend an account, make a POST request to the Account's instance URL `https://api.twilio.com/2010-04-01/Accounts/<account SID>.json`, posting the Status parameter with the suspended value.

In the PHP library, suspending an account looks like this:

```
$account = $client->accounts->get("<subaccount SID>");
$account->update(array("Status" => "suspended"));
```

If you want to "unsuspend" the account later, simply make a request to set its Status parameter to active.

Closing an account

Closing an account is an almost identical process. Simply make a request to set its Status parameter to closed.

This is more final than suspending an account in that it will be cut off permanently, will incur no further costs, and will not be able to be reopened.

All phone numbers that belong to it will be released, although historical records on the account will indefinitely remain accessible using its SID.

Usage

Naturally, running a Twilio account will incur costs from making and receiving calls and SMSes, which is on top of the running charges for operating phone numbers.

We can view this information manually from our Twilio account at `https://www.`
`twilio.com/user/account/usage/primary`. Fortunately, Twilio also provides
some really helpful APIs in order to keep track of and manage your expenses,
helping you build your own analytics and reporting tools.

 Twilio's Usage APIs are particularly useful when used with
subaccounts (described earlier), making it easy to track what
you should be billing your customers if you're offering a
service that makes use of Twilio.

Usage data is available for all of the different types of paid services Twilio offers,
from phone numbers to SMS messages to short codes to calls.

The data includes what was actually used in numerical terms—`Usage`, which might,
for instance, be in minutes or messages—and the monetary Cost.

Usage is split into a number of key categories, and many of these can be narrowed
down further. For example, `calls` is made up of six other categories including
`calls-sip` and `calls-client`:

Category	Description
`calls`	Voice calls
`sms`	SMS and MMS messages
`phonenumbers`	Incoming phone numbers
`recordings`	Recordings of voice calls
`transcriptions`	Transcriptions of voice calls
`totalprice`	Aggregated records covering all kinds of usage

Once we know what category we're looking at, we can then filter by date, specifying
a start and end date.

For instance, we might want to look up all calls during August 2014. To do
this, we'd make a GET request to `https://api.twilio.com/2010-04-01/`
`Accounts/<account SID>/Usage/Records.json`, specifying a `Category` of `calls`,
a `StartDate` of `2014-08-01`, and an `EndDate` of `2014-08-31`. Twilio will return a
series of usage records from which we can read totals and costs.

Working with the PHP library, we'd do the following:

```
foreach($client->account->usage_records->getIterator(0, 50, array(
  "Category" => "calls",
  "StartDate" => "2014-08-01",
  "EndDate" => "2014-08-31",
)) as $record) {
  echo $record->price;
}
```

> With the API, Twilio provides a few simpler ways to return records for particular time periods without working directly with dates (for example, to request yesterday's records or all records divided into months).
>
> There's too much content to cover here, but see the Twilio docs at https://www.twilio.com/docs/api/rest/usage-records#list-subresources for details.

On top of these basic read-only reporting functions, Twilio also provides powerful **Usage Triggers** where Twilio will ping you when you reach certain thresholds.

For instance, you might have an expectation for a certain expenditure by one of your users in a day on SMS messages, where behavior outside of this would suggest fraud or misuse. Usage Triggers make this easy to keep track of.

To create a new trigger, provide the following parameters:

Key	Description
UsageCategory (required)	This refers to the category to be monitored – see the categories used for usage records (earlier).
TriggerValue (required)	This refers to the value that, when hit, should trigger a callback to the specified URL.
TriggerBy	This refers to the value that should be monitored, either count, usage, or price (defaults to usage). See https://www.twilio.com/docs/api/rest/usage-records#usage-count-price for details on what these mean.
CallbackUrl (required)	This refers to the URL that Twilio should ping when the trigger is activated.
FriendlyName	This refers to a human-readable description for the trigger.
Recurring	This key sets whether this trigger should run once (default) or be reset on a regular basis (daily, monthly, or yearly).

Key	Description
CallbackMethod	This refers to the HTTP method Twilio should use when hitting your callback URL, which is either GET or POST (the default).

For instance, to set up a trigger for when more than 500 SMSes are sent by an account in any one day, we'd make a POST request to https://api.twilio.com/2010-04-01/Accounts/<account SID>/Usage/Triggers.json with a UsageCategory parameter of sms, TriggerValue parameter set to 500, a CallbackUrl parameter of our choice, and Recurring parameter specified as daily.

Using the PHP library, trigger would look like this:

```
$trigger = $client->account->usage_triggers->create("sms", "500",
"http://assets.twiliobestpractices.com/path/to/sms/trigger",
array("Recurring" => "daily"));
echo $trigger->sid;
```

A trigger, as with all Twilio REST API objects, has an SID. This means that we can easily load it later as well as change or delete it. We'll also be able to see our new trigger and edit and delete it from the Twilio website in the Usage section at https://www.twilio.com/user/account/usage/triggers.

Summary

In this chapter, we learned what the REST API is, including details on authentication and the different kinds of API requests you can make. We also saw how to get started with the PHP library (as well as how to find the libraries for other languages).

Alongside the API libraries, we interacted directly with the API using Postman, which is a great Chrome app, to get more down and dirty with the barebones of the API.

We mastered the Calls and Messages API and saw how we can use the various Phone Number APIs as well as the Subaccounts and *Usage* APIs to make our applications even more powerful.

In the next chapter, we'll look at the innovative Twilio Client tool, which enables you to make calls within your browser (or mobile app), removing physical phone hardware from the equation.

3
Calling in the Browser with Twilio Client

In this chapter, you'll cover the following topics:

- What Twilio Client is
- How it works at a high level
- Adding Twilio Client support to your backend, with PHP code examples
- Integrating Twilio Client into your web applications with JavaScript
- Getting started with the native Twilio Client for iOS and Android

What is Twilio Client?

The Twilio platform began as a way to provide easy connectivity between applications and **Public Switched Telephone Network (PSTN)** lines, that is, physical or real phones.

Twilio Client was launched in 2011, allowing you to take calls purely within a browser with no other hardware, abstracting away traditional telephony infrastructure and offering an experience similar to making a call through Skype or another VoIP service.

Not only can you enable your users to receive and make calls in their browser or your app to and from PSTN lines, but Twilio Client also allows calls between VoIP clients, enabling a massive range of rich voice-based experiences.

Originally, Twilio Client's VoIP worked through an Adobe Flash shim, but in modern browsers, it uses the WebRTC protocol (http://www.webrtc.org), offering better quality and compatibility.

On top of offering great new functionality, using the Client can also help you cut your telephony costs. Placing calls to Twilio Client users costs just 0.25 USD cents per minute, compared to the typical cost of 2 USD cents per minute to PSTN lines within the USA.

Where can I use Twilio Client?

In this chapter, we'll focus on using Twilio Client within your clients' browsers with Twilio's JavaScript plugin, Twilio.js (`https://www.twilio.com/docs/client/twilio-js`), alongside the Twilio PHP library we've already been playing with as a backend.

 You can check your web browser's compatibility with Twilio Client on Twilio's browser testing page at `http://clientsupport.twilio.com`.

We'll also briefly cover how to use the Client in native mobile apps, enabled by Twilio's provided libraries for iOS (`https://www.twilio.com/docs/client/ios`) and Android (`https://www.twilio.com/docs/client/android`). On mobile devices, your users can take calls wherever they are, using cellular (for example, 3G and 4G) and WiFi connections.

How does Twilio Client work?

There are four steps to follow when working with Twilio Client:

1. Setting it up with your credentials
2. Placing outgoing calls
3. Dealing with incoming calls
4. Interacting with calls currently in progress

Setting up the client

To get started, you'll use your language's Twilio API library to generate a **Capability Token**. This gives the client the right to make and/or receive calls using your account.

The following are embedded in this token:

- Your account credentials, ensuring that only you can give clients the right to make and receive calls using your Twilio credit

- The identifier that will be used to receive calls (if the client is allowed to receive calls)
- The Twilio application SID that will be used to place outgoing calls (if the client is allowed to place outgoing calls)

As an example, using the PHP library, we'll generate a Client token like this:

```
$accountSid = '<your account SID>';
$authToken  = '<your auth token>';
$capability = new Services_Twilio_Capability($accountSid, $authToken);
$capability->allowClientOutgoing('<your application SID>');
$capability->allowClientIncoming('your-choice-of-identifier');
$token = $capability->generateToken();
```

Placing outgoing calls

Placing an outgoing call with the Client requires you to set up a Twilio application, defining a TwiML URL that will be used to connect and handle your calls.

At first glance, it's quite natural here to ask, "Why can't I just enter a phone number and make the call?" There are a few reasons for this:

- **Security**: Passing your calls through some basic TwiML and thus the server-side code (for example, PHP) that powers it allows you to ensure that your Twilio credit isn't misused. For instance, without this, your users could potentially enter arbitrary phone numbers and call their friends using your money.

  Pinging your TwiML URL means that you can ensure that the user is performing a permitted operation, for instance, calling your customer support line, or connecting to another one of your other users in their browser.

- **Power**: Using TwiML means you get all of the power of TwiML that we've already seen in *Chapter 1, Working with TwiML*. Everything you've already seen is supported for Twilio Client users, from queues to conferences to call recordings. Anything you can do with a physical phone, you can do with an in-browser or in-app user.

In the previous PHP code sample, we specified the SID of an Application. As part of this Application record, we specify a Voice Request URL, and this will be pinged when a Client attempts to initiate a call, with any parameters we provide.

To create a TwiML App, head over to https://www.twilio.com/user/account/apps/add. For more detailed instructions, head to the end of *Chapter 1, Working with TwiML,* of this book.

When we initiate a call, we can pass in parameters based on user input, and these will be included in the request to our TwiML URL. For instance, we might specify a phone number we'd like to call, or the customer's account details to pass over to our support team when they're connected.

This data can be used to dynamically generate appropriate TwiML, for instance, <Dial> for dialing the appropriate physical phone number or Twilio Client, or reading out customized messages with the <Say> verb.

Receiving inbound calls

In the preceding PHP code sample, we set an identifier for incoming calls. This is what we'll use to ask Twilio to direct a call to the appropriate Client user.

When generating a token, we can choose to allow either inbound or outbound calls, or both, giving us fine-grained control over what our clients can do.

For this identifier, we are most likely to use a logged-in user's ID in our database, or some other uniquely identifiable piece of information.

From our TwiML, it's unbelievably simple to dial using a Client user's identifier rather than a PSTN phone number, using the <Client> noun instead of the <Number> noun:

```
<Dial>
  <Client>your-choice-of-identifier</Client>
</Dial>
```

When there's an incoming call, an **event** will be triggered on the Client's side, whether they're running JavaScript in a web browser or native code in an iOS or Android app.

As part of our code, we write an **event handler** to take the appropriate action to deal with an incoming call, whether it's displaying call details and an **Answer** button to the user, or automatically picking up the call (or in Twilio parlance, *accepting* it with the accept method) so that our user can speak right away.

Alongside the `incoming` event for calls that have come in and are ready to accept, Twilio Client libraries provide a number of other helpful events we can respond to, for instance, `connect` when a call actually begins or `presence` for when another one of your Client users goes online or offline, allowing you to build powerful real-time applications.

Full lists of events are available in the documentation for each individual library; for reference, see the JavaScript docs at `https://www.twilio.com/docs/client/device` and `https://www.twilio.com/docs/client/connection`.

Interacting with calls in progress

Once a call is in progress, you can interact with it using the `Connection` object that represents it.

These interactions work simply by calling methods on this `Connection` object. The following functions are available during a call:

Method name	Explanation
`disconnect`	This ends a call that is currently in progress
`mute`	This mutes (or unmutes) the call currently in progress; passing `true` as a parameter mutes it, and `false` unmutes it
`sendDigits`	This sends DTMF tones (that is, touch tone button presses) that are passed in, provided as a string containing characters 0-9, #, and *

Adding Twilio Client to your web applications

Let's start adding Twilio Client functionality to a real application with an in-depth tutorial, including complete HTML, JavaScript, and PHP code samples.

If you're not using PHP but rather another server-side language, the principles will be extremely similar. Simply see the Twilio *Capabilities* documentation for your own language. The JavaScript will remain the same irrespective of what you're running on your backend.

Suppose we add a page to our website that allows users to call our customer support team from within their browser. We'll let them choose the kind of problem they're having, and then we'll use that information to connect them to the right person.

Setting up a TwiML application

To place outgoing calls from a Twilio Client application, we need to set up a TwiML Application. This can be done via the API, as we saw in the previous chapter, but as this is most likely going to be a one-off task, we'll just do it from our Dashboard.

To get started, head to `https://www.twilio.com/user/account/apps/add`.

We'll call our application **In-Browser Customer Support** and enter a Voice Request URL, pointing to the PHP-powered `twiml.php` file we'll make a bit further into the chapter. Don't forget to set the HTTP method as appropriate. I'll stick with **HTTP GET**.

 You'll want to put in a URL and method such that your TwiML file will be accessible to Twilio from the Internet. This could be on some web hosting you own, or you could use the `ngrok` utility we tried in *Chapter 1, Working with TwiML*.

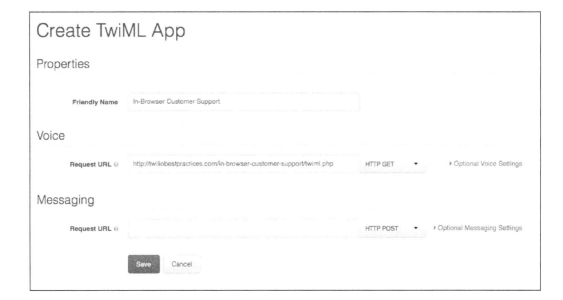

Hit **Save** and you'll be redirected to your list of applications. Click on **In-Browser Customer Support**, or whatever you named your application in the list, and then copy the **Sid** that starts with **AP** to your clipboard:

Building the frontend

Let's create the interface for our application. Create an `index.php` document and copy into it the following:

```
<!DOCTYPE html>
<html>
  <head>
    <meta charset="utf-8">
    <title>Contact Customer Support</title>
    <link rel="stylesheet" href="//cdnjs.cloudflare.com/ajax/libs/
    normalize/3.0.1/normalize.min.css" />
    <link rel="stylesheet" href="client.css" />
  </head>
  <body>
    <h1>Call our customer support team</h1>
    <div class="controls">
      <div class="client-status">
        Not yet ready.
      </div>
      <p><button class="hang-up">Hang up</a></button>
    </div>
    <h2>How can we help you?</h2>
    <p>Choose an option and we'll connect you to an agent right
    away.</p>
    <button class="call" data-customer-support
    option="billing">Billing</button>
    <button class="call" data-customer-support-option="tech">Technical
    support</button>
```

```
        <button class="call" data-customer-support-option="sales">Sales</
        button>
        <script src="//static.twilio.com/libs/twiliojs/1.2/twilio.min.
        js"></script>
        <script src="//code.jquery.com/jquery-1.11.0.min.js"></script>
        <script src="//code.jquery.com/jquery-migrate-1.2.1.min.js">
        </script>
    </body>
</html>
```

In the same directory, create a `client.css` file where we'll place some simple styles for our application:

```
body {
  font-family: sans-serif;
  margin: 1em;
}
.controls {
  margin: 1em 0 1em 1em;
  font-weight: bold;
}
button.call {
  display: inline-block;
  margin: 1em 2em 1em 0;
  color: #000;
}
```

As you'll see, here we have a basic HTML page with a few key features:

- We've included the `Twilio.js` library. We'll be using this to actually make and receive calls by writing some simple JavaScript.

- Also included is **jQuery** (`http://jquery.org`), an extremely useful and popular JavaScript library that makes it easy to interact with the DOM to add interactivity to our pages, plus `jquery-migrate` that retains compatibility with some features of old versions of jQuery.

- There's a `<div>` tag with the `client-status` class. Here, we'll show the current state of Twilio Client (although we've not written any code to actually make this happen).

- Finally, we have three `<button>` tags that will be used to start a call. Embedded into the dialing buttons in the `data-customer-support-option` attribute is what we'll use later to direct calls to the appropriate place. We'll need to write event handlers to make these buttons do something.

Generating a client token

In order to be able to make calls from our page, we'll need to securely generate a Client Capability token. We can do this using the Twilio PHP library.

 If you've not set up the PHP library yet, take a look at the beginning of *Chapter 2, Exploring REST API*. You'll need to download it and include it in your code manually, or use a package manager, such as Composer, to automate this.

At the top of the `index.php` page in the previous code, before the `<!DOCTYPE html>` tag, add the following PHP, filling in your account SID, auth token, and application SID:

```php
<?php
// To start, you'll need to include the Twilio PHP library, and
particularly
// the Capability functionality. Replace this with the path to where
you have
// the library installed, or the autoload file if you're using
Composer.
require 'Services/Twilio/Capability.php';
// Add your own API credentials here - we'll need these to generate a
token
$accountSid = 'ACxxxxxxxxxxxxxxxxxxxxxxxxxxxxxxxx';
$authToken  = 'yyyyyyyyyyyyyyyyyyyyyyyyyyyyyyyy';
$capability = new Services_Twilio_Capability($accountSid, $authToken);
$capability->allowClientOutgoing('<your application SID, created
above>');
$token = $capability->generateToken();
?>
```

Here's what we're doing, line by line:

1. First, we include the `Capability.php` file from the PHP library. We don't need the rest of the library's functionality here. Depending on how you're managing your dependencies, the exact way you require this might differ.

2. Next, we store our account SID and auth token into variables. We'll need these to securely create a token.

3. After that, we instantiate a `Services_Twilio_Capability` object, using our account SID and auth token. We'll build on this object to create the token.

4. Now, we call `allowClientOutgoing`, passing in the SID of the application we created earlier. This will allow the user on this page to make outgoing calls that will be passed through our application's TwiML URL.

 Note that we haven't enabled incoming calls for this token. To do this, we'd call the `allowClientIncoming` method.

5. Finally, we turn our object into a string token, stored as `$token`. This is what we'll actually be using within our JavaScript later.

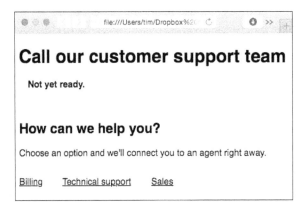

Powering our interactions with JavaScript

Now that we've written our PHP, let's do the fun part—writing some JavaScript to actually make our application do something.

Add a `<script>` tag at the bottom of your `index.php` document, just before the `</body>` tag, with the following:

```
<script>
    Twilio.Device.setup("<?php echo $token; ?>");
    Twilio.Device.ready(function(device) {
      $(".client-status").text("Ready.");
    });
    Twilio.Device.error(function(error) {
      console.debug(error);
      $(".client-status").text("Error: " + error.message);
    });
    Twilio.Device.connect(function(connection) {
      $(".client-status").text("Connected to customer support.");
      $("button.hang-up").css("visibility", "visible");
    });
```

```
Twilio.Device.disconnect(function(connection) {
  $(".client-status").text("Ready.");
  $("button.hang-up").css("visibility", "hidden");
});
$("button.call").on("click", function(event) {
  var option = $(this).attr("data-customer-support-option");
  Twilio.Device.connect({ option: option });
});
$("button.hang-up").on("click", function(event) {
  var connection = Twilio.Device.activeConnection();
  connection.disconnect();
});
</script>
```

There's a lot to get through and understand in the preceding code sample, so let's go through this block by block, explaining what each part does:

1. First, we call Twilio Client's `setup` method with the token we generated earlier in our PHP code, which we stored in `$token`. With our `echo` call, we inject the variable into our JavaScript.

2. Next, we set up a handler for Twilio Client's `ready` event. With this, the status indicator will start actually doing something. When Twilio Client is connected and ready to make and receive calls, it'll call the function we provide, which sets the status text to say `Ready`.

3. After this, we add a handler for error handling. We'll dump the full content of the error to our browser's JavaScript console and update our status to show what has gone wrong.

4. Next, we add two more handlers, `connect` and `disconnect`, which fire when a call starts and ends respectively. In our handler functions, we change the status message and toggle the visibility of our **Hang up** button (which is hidden by default thanks to our CSS, which we used earlier). We use `visibility` rather than actually showing and hiding using the jQuery built-in methods, so the page doesn't jump up and down when we show and hide things.

5. We then set up our various call buttons for different departments using some jQuery. When their `click` event fires, our function is called that grabs the name of the department from the clicked link's `data-customer-support-option` attribute, and then we start a new call with `Twilio.Device.connect`, passing in the department we want to call as the `option` parameter.

6. Finally, we wire up our **Hang up** button; when clicked, this finds the current Client connection (that is, call) and then disconnects it. The status field will be changed and the button itself will be hidden automatically, thanks to the disconnect handler we've already written.

Adding the TwiML

The magic is now there to make our page work, but one thing is missing: the TwiML to drive the call.

When we set up our TwiML application earlier from Twilio Dashboard, we specified a `twiml.php` file that should be used for outgoing calls. Create this `twiml.php` file, and put the following into it:

```php
<?php
    header("content-type: text/xml");
    echo "<?xml version=\"1.0\" encoding=\"UTF-8\"?>\n";
?>
<Response>
    <?php if ($_GET['option'] == "billing") { ?>
      <Say>We'll now connect you to our billing team.</Say>
    <?php } elseif ($_GET['option'] == "tech") { ?>
      <Say>We'll now connect you to our technical support team.</Say>
    <?php } elseif ($_GET['option'] == "sales") { ?>
      <Say>We'll now connect you to our sales team.</Say>
    <?php } else { ?>
      <Say>We didn't recognise your option, so we'll put you through
      to our switchboard.</Say>
    <?php } ?>
    <Play>http://com.twilio.sounds.music.s3.amazonaws.com/
    ClockworkWaltz.mp3</Play>
    <Hangup />
</Response>
```

Let's go through our TwiML file step by step:

1. First, we send the relevant headers for an XML file using PHP's `header` function. This isn't vital, but is good practice, and this means that we'll be representing our file correctly to clients who request it.

2. Next, we send an opening XML tag, which is again part of the correct format for an XML file.

3. Now, we build the meat and bones of our TwiML. We use conditional logic to change the output based upon the contents of `$_GET['option']`. You'll notice that the values we test come from the `data-customer-support-option` attribute on our HTML page: as we passed these in when calling `Twilio.Device.connect`, they are fed through to our TwiML in the request body.

4. Next, we play a slightly different message, depending on the department the user wants to speak to.

5. Next, we play some music. In the real world, we'd dial the appropriate number or join the customer to a queue, for instance.

6. Finally, we hang up; goodbye!

Make sure the `twiml.php` file is available at the URL specified when creating the Twilio application earlier, and we'll be ready to go.

Our very first Twilio Client call

Head to the index page, and you'll see the interface appear. All being well, the status indicator will change to **Ready**. Click on one of the department options, and a call will be started.

The first time you do this, you'll have to give Twilio Client permission to use your microphone. This will either be in the form of a (rather awkward) Flash settings pop-up, or if you're using Chrome or some other more up-to-date browser, an alert below the address bar:

Accept this, and your call will be connected, after Twilio Client plays its built-in connecting sound. You'll hear the message we entered into our `<Say>` verb, customized for the chosen department, plus the indicator will change and the **Hang up** button will appear:

Call our customer support team

Connected to customer support.

Hang up

While the music is playing, hang up. You've now got an application that can make outgoing calls using Twilio Client and is ready to be customized with whatever other options and TwiML you need.

Receiving incoming calls in the browser

We've now made an outgoing phone call from within the browser, but we're yet to see how receiving a call works.

To demonstrate this, let's build a page where our imaginary technical support team can take calls from customers in their browsers.

In the same directory as before, create a PHP file called `tech.php` that should contain the following:

```php
<?php
// To start, you'll need to include the Twilio PHP library, and
particularly
// the Capability functionality. Replace this with the path to where
you have
// the library installed, or the autoload file if you're using
Composer.
require 'Services/Twilio/Capability.php';
// Add your own API credentials here - we'll need these to generate a
token
$accountSid = '<your account SID>';
$authToken  = '<your auth token>';
$capability = new Services_Twilio_Capability($accountSid, $authToken);
$capability->allowClientIncoming("techsupport");
$token = $capability->generateToken();
?>
<!DOCTYPE html>
<html>
  <head>
    <meta charset="utf-8">
    <title>Technical Support call center</title>
    <link rel="stylesheet" href="//cdnjs.cloudflare.com/ajax/libs/
    normalize/3.0.1/normalize.min.css" />
    <link rel="stylesheet" href="client.css" />
  </head>
  <body>
    <h1>Technical Support call center</h1>
    <div class="controls">
      <div class="client-status">
        Not yet ready.
      </div>
      <p><button class="hang-up">Hang up</button></p>
    </div>
    <p>When a call comes in, you'll receive a popup, allowing you to
    accept the call if you're available.</p>
```

```
    <script src="//static.twilio.com/libs/twiliojs/1.2/
    twilio.min.js"></script>
    <script src="//code.jquery.com/jquery-1.11.0.min.js"></script>
    <script src="//code.jquery.com/jquery-migrate-1.2.1.min.js">
    </script>
  </body>
</html>
```

Let's go through this briefly, and as you'll see, most of it is very similar to what we used in our previous backend code to allow customers to make calls:

- First, we set up our Twilio Client with our account SID and auth token, creating a Client token, but this time setting it up to receive calls to the techsupport identifier. The browser will register itself with Twilio using this name, and we'll use it to connect calls to this browser.

- We include core libraries, such as Twilio.js and jQuery, and use the same client.css file as before, sharing our look and feel.

- We hold on to the status indicator and **Hang up** button from before, but replace the list of departments with a simple paragraph of text.

Now, let's add some JavaScript in a <script> tag just before the </body> tag to handle our incoming calls:

```
<script>
    Twilio.Device.setup("<?php echo $token; ?>");
    Twilio.Device.ready(function(device) {
      $(".client-status").text("Ready.");
    });
    Twilio.Device.error(function(error) {
      console.debug(error);
      $(".client-status").text("Error: " + error.message);
    });
    Twilio.Device.connect(function(connection) {
      $(".client-status").text("Connected to customer.");
      $("button.hang-up").css("visibility", "visible");
    });
    Twilio.Device.disconnect(function(connection) {
      $(".client-status").text("Ready.");
      $("button.hang-up").css("visibility", "hidden");
    });
    Twilio.Device.incoming(function(connection) {
      if (confirm('Would you like to accept the incoming call?')) {
        connection.accept();
      }
```

```
        });
        $("a.hang-up").on("click", function(event) {
            var connection = Twilio.Device.activeConnection();
            connection.disconnect();
        });
    </script>
```

This is very similar to the JavaScript we used for our previous frontend with the same line of code to set up the client, many of the same handlers, and an identically wired-up **Hang up** button.

The main addition here is that we've added a handler for the `incoming` event, which is triggered when there is an incoming call.

When Twilio lets us know about an incoming call, we display a popup, and if the user accepts the call, it is connected. As before, we rely on the `connect` handler to make the required changes to the interface when a call begins successfully.

Everything is ready to go, but we need some way to actually get calls into this otherwise closed system. Let's go back to our `twiml.php` file and use a `<Dial>` verb to call our technical support agents in their browsers instead of playing music:

```
<?php
    header("content-type: text/xml");
    echo "<?xml version=\"1.0\" encoding=\"UTF-8\"?>\n";
?>
<Response>
    <?php if ($_GET['option'] == "billing") { ?>
        <Say>We'll now connect you to our billing team.</Say>
        <Play>http://com.twilio.sounds.music.s3.amazonaws.com/
        ClockworkWaltz.mp3</Play>
    <?php } elseif ($_GET['option'] == "tech") { ?>
        <Say>We'll now connect you to our technical support team.</Say>
        <Dial>
          <Client>techsupport</Client>
        </Dial>
    <?php } elseif ($_GET['option'] == "sales") { ?>
        <Say>We'll now connect you to our sales team.</Say>
        <Play>http://com.twilio.sounds.music.s3.amazonaws.com/
        ClockworkWaltz.mp3</Play>
    <?php } else { ?>
        <Say>We didn't recognise your option, so we'll put you through
        to our switchboard.</Say>
```

```
        <Play>http://com.twilio.sounds.music.s3.amazonaws.com/
        ClockworkWaltz.mp3</Play>
      <?php } ?>
      <Hangup />
   </Response>
```

To place a call to our Twilio Client users, we use the `<Dial>` verb with a `<Client>` noun inside, specifying the identifier we want to call. We set this identifier with our earlier call to `allowClientIncoming` in our PHP code.

Now that everything is together, let's try our completed application. Open `index.php` in one browser and `tech.php` in another.

On the **Call our customer support team** page, click on **Technical support**. After a few seconds, you'll get a popup in your other browser window asking you to accept the call:

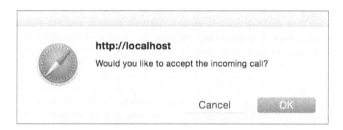

Once you've accepted, speak into your microphone, and you'll hear it played back from your speakers. Magical!

Clearly, what we've seen here is a bare-bones implementation of incoming calls. There's plenty you might want to add, from time indicators to keypads to generally sprucing up the interface. Fortunately, building on the fundamentals you've already seen, adding all of these things is relatively easy.

Getting started with Twilio Client on iOS and Android

As well as working in web browsers using JavaScript, Twilio Client can also be integrated into native apps for iOS and Android, thanks to Twilio's SDKs for the two platforms.

The structure of these integrations is very similar to what we've already seen. The frontend, that is, the application itself, provides an interface, with a backend server generating tokens and serving up TwiML.

Capability tokens are generated on a server rather than on the client's device so that you don't have to share your account SID and auth token. This keeps your Twilio credit safe and under your control.

You'll always need a server that creates tokens when clients request for them. This might be written in PHP, or any other language for which Twilio provides an API library. You can even use the code we've already written.

The Client APIs for Android and iOS are very similar to what we've already seen in JavaScript, reusing concepts such as Connection and Device and extensively using event handlers. In your application, you'll:

- Contact your server to request a Capability Token
- Bind handlers to Twilio Client events, such as connect, ready and error, as well as incoming if you want to take incoming calls
- Create an interface for making, receiving, and managing calls, where user interactions are bound to particular functions

Fully explaining and providing code samples for iOS and Android is out of the scope of this book, which is focused on in-browser applications. However, Twilio provides extensive documentation and tutorials to help you get started.

To get up and running, start with Twilio's getting started tutorials at `https://www.twilio.com/docs/quickstart/ios-client` for iOS and `https://www.twilio.com/docs/quickstart/php/android-client` for Android.

Summary

In this chapter, we covered the fundamentals of the Twilio Client: what it is and how it works at a high level, before integrating it into a PHP application in the browser for both incoming and outgoing calls with full code samples.

We also briefly considered how to use Twilio Client in a mobile app for iOS or Android.

In the next chapter, we'll put together what we've already learned, building two exciting projects using the Twilio platform: a "request a callback" tool for your website and a conference calling service.

4
Twilio in the Real World

In this chapter, you'll use the skills you've already gained in the first three chapters to build the following two great projects on the Twilio platform with the PHP API library:

- A callback request tool for your website
- A simple conference calling service

The callback request tool

First up, we're going to build a callback request tool that is suitable for any website.

Popular across the Internet, such tools are great for small businesses that want to let their customers get in touch with them without the annoying need to wait on hold.

There are four components of this tool:

1. A simple website with a form for collecting customer details
2. A PHP page that initiates a call to the customer who requested it when a member of staff clicks on a link
3. A short piece of TwiML to power this call
4. A status callback page that listens for a request from Twilio to let it know that a call was answered so the database can be updated

Let's get started.

Preparing the project

To start, we'll need to get some dependencies in order and prepare a configuration and setup file that can be included in all of our pages.

Installing the Twilio API library

First, we'll install the Twilio PHP library using Composer.

To do that, first install Composer on your machine (if you don't have it already) by heading to `https://getcomposer.org/doc/00-intro.md` and following the instructions.

Once Composer is installed, create a new directory for the callbacks tool and run the following:

```
composer require twilio/sdk
```

In the prompt that appears, enter `dev-master`, and then hit *Enter*. The Twilio PHP library will be installed, and an autoload file will be generated to make it easy to include this in your project.

Preparing the MySQL database

We'll store all of the callback requests we get in a MySQL database, persisting important details such as the customer's name and phone number, and whether they've been called back yet.

First up, you'll need to create a database. Give it any name you like and make sure you have a database user who can access that database.

Let's create a `requests` table with all of the fields we'll need. You can create the table by running this SQL (saved as `requests.sql` with the code samples) against your database. You'll need to make sure you've selected the database first:

```
CREATE TABLE IF NOT EXISTS `requests` (
  `id` int(11) NOT NULL AUTO_INCREMENT,
  `first_name` varchar(64) NOT NULL,
  `email` varchar(128) NOT NULL,
  `phone_number` varchar(32) NOT NULL,
  `status` varchar(16) NOT NULL DEFAULT 'pending',
  PRIMARY KEY (`id`)
) ENGINE=InnoDB DEFAULT CHARSET=latin1 AUTO_INCREMENT=1 ;
```

Creating a configuration file

Now, let's put together a configuration file that will share basic pieces of configuration between files plus the initialization of the MySQL connection and Twilio API library.

Create a file called `config.inc.php` and place the following in it:

```php
<?php
// Include Composer's autoload file to bring in the Twilio library
// require('vendor/autoload.php');
$settings = array(
  "mysql_host" => "<your MySQL server host
  (probably'127.0.0.1')>",
  "mysql_username" => "<your MySQL username>",
  "mysql_password" => "<your MySQL password>",
  "mysql_database" => "<your MySQL database's name,
  which you created earlier>",
  "from_email" => "<email to send emails to our agents from>",
  "root_url" => "<URL to the directory of your project,
  accessible from the Internet>",
  "twilio_sid" => "<Your Twilio SID>",
  "twilio_auth_token" => "<Your Twilio auth token>",
  "twilio_caller_id" => "<The caller ID to use for
  outgoing calls>",
  // Replace these with your own agents, following the same
  //format. Each one
  // will receive an email when there's a new callback request.
  "agents" => array(
    "Tim" => array(
      "phone_number" => "+447800200100",
      "email" => "tim@twiliobestpractices.com"
    ),
    "Kit" => array(
      "phone_number" => "+447800100200",
      "email" => "kit@twiliobestpractices.com"
    )
  )
);
$db = new mysqli(
  $settings["mysql_host"],
  $settings["mysql_username"],
  $settings["mysql_password"],
  $settings["mysql_database"]
);
if ($db->connect_error) {
  die("Something went wrong whilst connecting to the database: " .
  $db->connect_error);
}
$twilio = new Services_Twilio($settings["twilio_sid"],
$settings["twilio_auth_token"]);
?>
```

You'll now need to go through the `$settings` variable, filling in the placeholders. Here are some quick instructions that will be of help:

1. In the `root_url` setting, enter the URL where your code will be accessible from the Internet with a trailing forward slash. For example, if `config. inc.php` will be stored at `http://twiliobestpractices.com/callbacks/ config.inc.php`, you should add `http://twiliobestpractices.com/ callbacks/` there.

2. Fill in the `twilio_caller_id` setting with either a phone number you've bought through Twilio or one you've already verified as a caller ID.

3. Update `$agents` with a couple of entries using e-mails and phone numbers you have access to.

Creating the request form

Let's get going with building the interface where users will enter their name, e-mail, and phone number to request a callback.

To start, let's create a `style.css` file in our project directory with some simple styles that will make our page look a lot nicer with very little work:

```css
body {
    margin: 2em;
    color: #777;
    line-height: 2em;
}
h1 {
    color: #000;
}
ul.parsley-errors-list {
    list-style-type: none;
}
p.error {
    margin-left: 2em;
    font-weight: bold;
    font-style: italic;
}
```

Now, we'll jump straight in and create our `index.php` file. This will contain the form itself:

```php
<!DOCTYPE html>
<html>
    <head>
```

```
  <meta charset="utf-8">
    <title>Request a callback</title>
    <link rel="stylesheet"
    href="http://yui.yahooapis.com/pure/0.5.0/pure-min.css" />
    <link rel="stylesheet" href="style.css" />
  </head>
  <body>
    <h1>Request a callback</h1>
    <p>Enter your details below, and a member of the team will contact
you as soon
      as possible.</p>
    <?php if (isset($_GET['incomplete'])) { ?>
      <p class="error">
        You didn't fill in all the fields. Please try again.</p>
      </p>
    <?php } ?>
    <form action="create.php" method="POST" class="pure-form pure-
    form-stacked" data-persist="garlic" data-destroy="false" data-
parsley-validate>
      <fieldset>
        <label for="first_name">First name</label>
        <input name="first_name" type="text" placeholder="Tim"
        required autofocus />
        <label for="email">Email</label>
        <input name="email" type="email"
        placeholder="tim@twiliobestpractices.com" required />

        <label for="phone_number">Phone number</label>
        <input name="phone_number" type="tel"
placeholder="+441290211999" required data-parsley-
pattern="^\+?\d{10,15}$" />
        <p>If you're in the US, you can enter your number as
        normal. Otherwise,
        please enter it in international format.</p>

        <input type="submit" value="Call me" class="pure-button
        pure-button-primary" />
      </fieldset>
    </form>

<script src="//code.jquery.com/jquery-1.11.0.min.js"></script>
    <script src="//code.jquery.com/jquery-migrate-
    1.2.1.min.js"></script>
    <script src="//cdnjs.cloudflare.com/ajax/libs/
    parsley.js/2.0.5/parsley.min.js"></script>
```

```
<script src="//cdnjs.cloudflare.com/ajax/libs/garlic.js/
1.2.2/garlic.min.js"></script>

</body>
</html>
```

Let's go through this to understand it a little better:

1. First, we include some external dependencies alongside our own `style.css`
   file that will help us make our project look and feel great with no effort at all:

   ○ **Pure**: This is a CSS library created by Yahoo that will make our forms
     look pretty. Refer to `http://purecss.io`.

   ○ **Parsley**: This is an open source JavaScript library by Guillaume Potier
     (`https://twitter.com/guillaumepotier`) that makes client-side
     form validations simple. Refer to `http://parsleyjs.org`.

   ○ **Garlic**: This is another open source JS library for automatically
     remembering a user's form inputs, making their life a little easier.
     Refer to `http://garlicjs.org`.

2. Next, we start the body. Just inside it, we include an error message that will
   be displayed if `?incomplete=true` is tacked onto the end of the URL. This
   is something we'll trigger from the form's action where required.

3. In the `<form>` tag itself, we use some special classes to activate Pure's form
   styles plus a couple of `data-` attributes to activate Garlic and Parsley.

4. We then have the form labels, fields, and the **Submit** button, with the form
   fields including attributes such as `required` and `data-parsley-format` to
   let Parsley know how to validate our form.

Now that our form is looking pretty, let's build the action behind it in `create.php`:

```php
<?php
include('config.inc.php');
$first_name = $_POST['first_name'];
$email = $_POST['email'];
$phone_number = $_POST['phone_number'];
if (!empty($first_name) && !empty($email) &&
!empty($phone_number)) {
  $statement = $db->prepare("INSERT INTO requests (first_name,
  email, phone_number) VALUES (?, ?, ?)");
  $statement->bind_param("sss", $first_name, $email,
  $phone_number);
  $statement->execute();
  $id = $statement->insert_id;
```

```php
$headers = "From: " . $settings["from_email"] . "\r\n";
$headers .= "MIME-Version: 1.0\r\n";
$headers .= "Content-Type: text/html; charset=ISO-8859-1\r\n";
foreach ($settings["agents"] as $agent_name => $agent_details) {
  $message = "<p>Hi " . $agent_name . ",</p>
  <p>" . $first_name . " has just requested a callback on " .
  $phone_number . "</p>" .
  "<p>To give him/her a call, click <a href='" .
  $settings["root_url"] .
  "call.php?id=" . $id . "&phone_number=" .
  $agent_details["phone_number"]
  . "'>here</a>." .
  "<p>Thanks!</p>";
  mail($agent_details["email"], "New callback request (#" .
  $id . ")", $message, $headers);
  }
} else {
  header("Location: index.php?incomplete=true");
  }
?>
<!DOCTYPE html>
<html>
  <head>
    <title>Thanks! | Request a callback</title>
    <link rel="stylesheet"
    href="http://yui.yahooapis.com/pure/0.5.0/pure-min.css" />
    <link rel="stylesheet" href="style.css" />
  </head>
  <body>
    <h1>Thanks <?php echo $first_name; ?></h1>
    <p>We'll call you as soon as possible.</p>
  </body>
</html>
```

Now, I'll take you through this code:

1. First, we bring in our `config.inc.php` file—simple!

2. Next, we check whether a first name, e-mail, and phone number have been provided. If not, we redirect the user back to the `index.php` file with the `incomplete` URL parameter set, thereby activating the error message we saw earlier.

3. Next, we insert our request into the database. To do this, we construct a query using the `prepare` method with question marks (?) to represent placeholders in the query. We then use the `bind_param` method to replace these placeholders with our real data in a secure way that minimizes the likelihood of security vulnerabilities, before actually running the query to insert the record.

4. After this, we loop through the agents we specified in our configuration, sending each of them an e-mail with a personalized link to connect this callback request to their own number.

5. Finally, we display a **thank you** message to the person requesting the callback, personalized with their own name.

Responding to a callback request from an e-mail

In the e-mail, we refer to a new file called `call.php`. Let's create it now. When clicked on, it'll initiate the call between the agent who received the e-mail and the end user:

```
<!DOCTYPE html>
<html>
  <head>
    <title>Dialing... | Request a callback</title>
    <link rel="stylesheet"
    href="http://yui.yahooapis.com/pure/0.5.0/pure-min.css" />
    <link rel="stylesheet" href="style.css" />
  </head>
  <body>
    <?php
    include('config.inc.php');
    $id = $_GET['id'];
    $phone_number = $_GET['phone_number'];
    if (!empty($id) && !empty($phone_number)) {
      $statement = $db->prepare("SELECT * FROM requests
      WHERE id = ?");
      $statement->bind_param("i", $id);
      $statement->execute();
      $result = $statement->get_result();
      if ($result) {
        $request = $result->fetch_assoc();
        if ($request["status"] != "pending") {
          include('includes/already_called.php');
        } else {
```

```
            $twilio->account->calls->create(
              $settings["twilio_caller_id"],
              $phone_number,
              $settings["root_url"] . "twiml.php?id=" . $id,
              array()
            );
            include('includes/connecting.php');
          }
        } else {
          include('includes/error.php');
        }
      } else {
        include('includes/error.php');
      }
      ?>
    </body>
</html>
```

This file is a little more complicated to deal with, considering all the possible conditions with lots of if and else statements. Let's go through these together:

- If we have an ID and phone number passed to the page in the URL (that is, the visitor has clicked on a valid link in an e-mail):
    - We load the callback request by its ID and store it in the $request variable.
    - If the person has already been called back (that is, the status in the database is not pending), we include the already_called.php file.
    - If the person still needs to be called back, we initiate a call using the Twilio API library to the agent's phone number (passed in through the URL), pointing Twilio to TwiML in twiml.php and passing the ID of the callback request, before including connecting.php.

- If an ID and phone number wasn't provided, or the record couldn't be found, we display error.php.

I chose to separate the various messages into their own files to make the code cleaner and easier to read. Let's create those files now.

Start by creating an includes/ directory, and then we'll create connecting.php in it:

```
<h1>Thanks!</h1>
<p>We'll call you now, and connect the customer in.</p>
```

...and then, `already_called.php`:

```
<h1>Too late!</h1>
<p>This request has already been called back.</p>
```

...and finally, `error.php`:

```
<h1>Oops, something went wrong.</h1>
<p>Please click a valid link from an email.</p>
```

Writing the TwiML

Let's write `twiml.php`, which Twilio will use when one of our agents responds to a callback:

```php
<?php
    include('config.inc.php');
    $id = $_GET['id'];
    $statement = $db->prepare("SELECT * FROM requests
    WHERE id = ?");
    $statement->bind_param("i", $id);
    $statement->execute();
    $result = $statement->get_result();
    if ($result) { $request = $result->fetch_assoc(); }
    header("content-type: text/xml");
    echo "<?xml version=\"1.0\" encoding=\"UTF-8\"?>\n";
?>
<Response>
  <?php if ($request) { ?>
    <Say>You're now being connected to <?php echo
    $request["first_name"]; ?>.</Say>
    <Dial callerId="<?php echo $settings["twilio_caller_id"]; ?>"
    action="status_callback.php?id=<?php echo $id; ?>">
      <Number><?php echo $request["phone_number"]; ?></Number>
    </Dial>
  <?php } else { ?>
    <Say>Oops, something went wrong. Goodbye.</Say>
    <Hangup />
  <?php } ?>
</Response>
```

Here, we do the following:

- Grab the ID from the URL and use it to select the reservation request from the database.
- Send the relevant XML headers and opening lines.

- If the request was loaded successfully, we:
    - Play a short message to the agent being called with the name of the person they're about to speak to.
    - Dial the requester's number, with the appropriate caller ID and an action specified (we'll use it shortly to listen for whether the call was successful).

- If the request couldn't be found, we play an error message and hang up.

Listening for a call's status

On the `<Dial>` verb in our preceding TwiML, we specify an action. This means that when the call finishes Twilio will make a request to that path, which is `status_callback.php`, with a `DialCallStatus` parameter indicating whether the call was successful.

Let's finish up by creating `status_callback.php`:

```php
<?php
include('config.inc.php');
$id = $_GET['id'];
if (!empty($id) && $_REQUEST['DialCallStatus'] == "completed") {
    $statement = $db->prepare("UPDATE requests SET status =
    'completed' WHERE id = ?");
    $statement->bind_param("i", $id);
    $statement->execute();
}
header("content-type: text/xml");
echo "<?xml version=\"1.0\" encoding=\"UTF-8\"?>\n";
?>
<Response>
  <Say>Thank you, and goodbye.</Say>
  <Hangup />
</Response>
```

Here, we:

- Update the request's `status` in the database to `completed` if the call was successful (that is, the customer picked up).
    - In the `call.php` file we created earlier to allow the agent to respond to a callback, we checked this status to determine whether a call should be placed or the agent is too late.

- Respond with some simple TwiML for anyone still on the line, saying goodbye and hanging up.

Wrapping up

Using PHP, a MySQL database, and the Twilio API, we've built a callback request tool. Customers can request a callback, dispatching an e-mail to us so that we can call them back in one click. We then record in the database once the customer has been called back successfully.

The conference calling tool

Secondly, we're going to build a simple conference calling tool, which is suitable for any small business or organization. Ours will be virtually free to run, requiring just a little Twilio credit and somewhere to host our PHP, and it will support great features such as call recording.

There are three components to this tool:

- A simple website with a **Create, Read, Update, Delete (CRUD)** interface to manage our conference calls.
- TwiML to handle incoming calls and dial them in to the correct conference.
- An endpoint to listen for Twilio's callback with the URL of a recording of our conference.

Let's get started.

Preparing the project

We'll need to get our dependencies set up, and then we'll be ready to start writing some real code.

This time around, we're going to work with a PHP framework called **Laravel** (`http://laravel.com`). Laravel is a PHP framework for web artisans, which moves us away from individual PHP files for each page (like we've seen previously) towards a more structured, and ultimately much more maintainable, application.

If you've never used an **Model View Controller** (**MVC**) framework before, then there'll be a learning curve in this project for you. Stick to it as I take you through the project and explain what's going on. Once you've built applications this way, you'll never go back.

MVC is a pattern for application design that separates our code into three main elements: the model that interacts with the database, the controller that handles inbound requests, and the view that presents data to the user. For a primer on MVC, refer to `http://code.tutsplus.com/tutorials/mvc-for-noobs--net-10488`.

Setting up your environment

Hosting your Laravel application can be a bit confusing at first, since doing so has quite specific requirements. To get around this, let's use a tool called **Laravel Homestead**, which sets up a virtual machine on your computer with everything you need, including PHP, MySQL, and an nginx web server, and hosts your code for you.

To get set up, head to `http://laravel.com/docs/4.2/homestead`, and just follow the instructions. First, you'll install VirtualBox (a virtualization product created by Oracle), then you'll install Vagrant (a command-line tool for managing our virtual machines), and then you'll install the Homestead box itself.

Follow all of the steps on the previous page, sharing the folder where you keep your programming projects with your virtual machine and creating a site for your application by editing `Homestead.yaml`, somewhat like what is shown in the following code, of course replacing the paths in the `map` keys with the locations of your `Projects` and `conferences` directories (we'll set up the conferences directory in the next section):

```
folders:
    - map: /Users/tim/Projects
      to: /home/vagrant/Projects
sites:
    - map: conferences.app
      to: /home/vagrant/Projects/conferences/public
```

Once you've edited the configuration, run `vagrant up` from your Homestead directory to start your virtual machine. All being well, when you go to `http://localhost:8000`, you'll be greeted with a Laravel welcome page.

You can follow the full tutorial on `http://laravel.com/docs/4.2/homestead`, to get up and running.

Setting up Laravel

Creating your first Laravel project is easy, and we can get started using Composer, which is already installed on our new Homestead virtual machine.

From the Homestead directory, run `vagrant ssh` to log in to the machine. Next, navigate to the directory where you keep your projects (in the previous `Vagrantfile` example, this would be `/home/vagrant/projects`), and then run the following command:

```
composer create-project laravel/laravel conferences --prefer-dist
```

This will ask Composer to create a Laravel project called `conferences` in a `conferences` directory.

Next, let's add another useful package called Validating (`https://github.com/dwightwatson/validating`). This package makes it easy for us to validate our models (that is, our data), for instance, ensuring that each of our conferences has a name. To do this, move to our new `conferences` directory and invoke Composer:

```
composer require "watson/validating:0.10.*"
```

Setting up our database

As we're using Homestead, all of our database configuration is set up automatically. We'll just need to write a **migration** to set up a table for our data.

If you've not used a framework before, migrations will probably be unfamiliar for you, but you've most likely used **phpMyAdmin** or a similar tool to create your database manually.

Migrations help keep things organized in a better way. They're an executable description of your database that can be used on any computer, at any time, to rebuild your database from scratch. They describe the tables, columns, constraints, and everything else about your database…apart from the data.

We can create a migration from the command line. To do so, make sure you're in your `conferences` directory while SSHed into the Homestead machine. Then, run the following:

```
php artisan migrate:make create_conferences_table
```

Laravel will create a template migration PHP file in the `app/database/migrations` directory for you. Its filename will contain the current date and time, plus the name we specified, which is `create_conferences_table`.

To make changes to our file, we can just use our normal text editor outside of our Vagrant SSH session. Our `conferences` directory is automatically synced between our desktop environment and the virtual machine, as specified in `Vagrantfile`.

In the migration file that has been created, change the `up()` method to the following:

```
Schema::create('conferences', function($table)
  {
  $table->increments('id');
    $table->string('name');
    $table->string('access_code')->unique();
    $table->boolean('active')->default(true);
    $table->string('recording_url');
    $table->timestamps();
  });
```

This file essentially describes the `conferences` table we'll use to store the conference calls we've organized. The `up()` method will be called when we want to make these changes to the database.

In the `up()` method, we specify that we want to create a table called `conferences`, and then we add all of our various columns to that, for instance, an auto-incrementing `id` column, a unique `access_code` column, and creation and update timestamps.

To make our migration reversible with `php artisan migrate:rollback`, add the following to the `drop()` method in the file:

```
Schema::drop("conferences");
```

Let's run our migration to make these updates to the database. To do this, we'll need to SSH into our Vagrant box. Use `cd` in the terminal to navigate to the `Homestead` directory, and then run `vagrant ssh`.

For the Homestead box, you'll be in a shell. Navigate to the `conferences` directory. If you need a reminder of where it is, refer to your `Homestead.yaml` file, and then run `php artisan migrate`. If asked, type **yes** to confirm, and the database will be updated.

Now, just run the `exit` command to end your SSH connection to the Homestead machine.

We've set up the database, so now we'll want to create a **model** using a library included with Laravel called **Eloquent**. This is a special kind of class that we'll use to interact with the database rather than using raw SQL queries.

Create a file in `app/models` called `Conference.php`, and type the following in it:

```php
<?php
use Watson\Validating\ValidatingTrait;
class Conference extends Eloquent {
  use ValidatingTrait;
  protected $table = 'conferences';
  protected $fillable = array('name');
  protected $rules = [
    'name' => 'required',
    'access_code' => 'numeric|unique:conferences'
  ];
  public function scopeActive($query) {
    return $query->where('active', '=', true);
  }
  public function scopeArchived($query) {
    return $query->where('active', '=', false);
  }
  public function generateAndSetAccessCode() {
    $access_code = mt_rand(100000, 999999);
    while (!Conference::active()->where('access_code', '=', $access_
code)->get()->isEmpty()) {
      $access_code = mt_rand(100000, 999999);
    }
    $this->access_code = $access_code;
  }
  public static function boot() {
    parent::boot();
    static::creating(function($conference) {
      $conference->generateAndSetAccessCode();
    });
  }
}
```

Let's go through this bit by bit:

1. We bring in `ValidatingTrait` from the Validating composer package we installed earlier. We then open up our `Conference` class, inheriting from the `Eloquent` class that includes all of the database functionality we need.

2. Next, we set some settings, telling Laravel to use the `conferences` table to store this model's data; to make the `name` field fillable (don't worry about what this means for now) and to set some validation rules for our object. For example, it must have a `name`, and its `access_code` must be numeric and unique.

3. After this, we specify some scopes, which are effectively reusable queries. This means we'll be able to use the `Conference::active()` and `Conference::archived()` methods to find active and inactive conferences, respectively, without writing any SQL at all. As you'll see, even when defining the scope, we use a Laravel abstraction of the usual raw SQL to set our `where` condition.

4. Now, we write our own custom functionality in the `generateAndSetAccessCode` method. This generates a six-digit number until it finds one that it is not already being used by another conference and then sets it on the model, making it ready to be saved to the database.

5. Finally, we override Eloquent's `boot()` method, which is called when an instance of our `Conference` class is instantiated. In this, we add a callback handler for whenever a conference is created (that is, saved to the database for the first time), generating an access code automatically.

Building the CRUD interface

Now that we've set up the database and written our model, let's build the interface we'll use to create and manage our conference calls.

As I mentioned, when using a framework such as Laravel, we don't use individual PHP files to represent each action (that is, the page) in our application. Instead, **controllers** are responsible for handling requests (for instance, manipulating data and loading things from the database) that are then handed off to views for display.

We route URLs to their appropriate controllers using the `app/routes.php` file. Open it up now, and replace the existing route with the following:

```
Route::get('/', array(
  'uses' => 'ConferencesController@index',
  'as' => 'conferences.index'
));
Route::get('/conferences/archived', array(
  'uses' => 'ConferencesController@archived',
  'as' => 'conferences.archived'
));
Route::get('/conferences/new', array(
  'as' => 'conferences.new',
  'uses' => 'ConferencesController@build'
));
Route::post('/conferences', array(
  'as' => 'conferences.create',
  'uses' => 'ConferencesController@create'
```

```
));
Route::get('/conferences/{id}', array(
  'as' => 'conferences.show',
  'uses' => 'ConferencesController@show'
));
Route::put('/conferences/{id}/archive', array(
  'as' => 'conferences.archive',
  'uses' => 'ConferencesController@archive'
));
Route::put('/conferences/{id}/unarchive', array(
  'as' => 'conferences.unarchive',
  'uses' => 'ConferencesController@unarchive'
));
Route::post('/conferences/{id}', array(
  'as' => 'conferences.update',
  'uses' => 'ConferencesController@update'
));
Route::delete('/conferences/{id}', array(
  'as' => 'conferences.destroy',
  'uses' => 'ConferencesController@destroy'
));
```

This might look slightly bewildering. In each block, we're doing a few things:

1. First, we specify the HTTP method this route responds to (GET, PUT, POST, or DELETE).

2. Next, we set the URL, sometimes including {id}, which acts as a placeholder for where the ID of a particular conference will appear in the URL.

3. Then, in the array, we set a name for the route (we can use this later to generate URLs without writing them ourselves) and we specify what controller and method should handle the request. For example, ConferencesController@ show refers to the show method on ConferencesController, and this method will be passed the ID from the URL where a placeholder has been included.

Now, we need to actually write our controller to deal with all of these requests! In the app/controllers directory, create a ConferencesController.php file and in it, place the following:

```php
<?php
class ConferencesController extends BaseController {
  public function index()
  {
    $conferences = Conference::active()->get();
```

```
        return View::make('conferences/index', array('conferences' =>
    $conferences));
      }
      public function archived()
      {
        $conferences = Conference::archived()->get();
        return View::make('conferences/archived', array('conferences' =>
    $conferences));
      }
    }
    ?>
```

This creates our first two pages, which will display active and archived conferences, respectively. In the methods, we use our `Conference` model's scope that we defined earlier to load the right records. We then create and return a view, passing the conferences we just loaded into it.

In the first argument of `View::make`, we provide the path to a view file. Let's create these two files now. Create an `index.blade.php` file in `app/views/conferences`:

```
@extends('layout')
@section('content')
  <h2>Conferences</h2>
  <ul>
    @foreach ($conferences as $conference)
      <li>{{ link_to_route('conferences.show', $conference->name,
array('id' => $conference->id)) }}</li>
    @endforeach
  </ul>
@stop
```

Here, we loop through our conferences that we passed into the view earlier, and then for each one, we display a list item that links to its individual `show` page.

In the **Blade** view templating language we're working with here, we include PHP calls in curly braces ({{ and }}).

 You can find the full documentation on working with Blade templates at `http://laravel.com/docs/4.2/templates`. It's a quick and very useful read.

The `link_to_route` function takes the name of a route (as specified in our `routes` file), the text to display and then an array of options, which are used to generate the URL. Here, we provide the conference's ID.

Now, create `archived.blade.php` in the same directory. This is very similar indeed:

```
@extends('layout')
@section('content')
  <h2>Archived conferences</h2>
  <ul>
    @foreach ($conferences as $conference)
       <li>{{ link_to_route('conferences.show', $conference->name,
array('id' => $conference->id)) }}</li>
    @endforeach
  </ul>
@stop
```

At the top of the view, you'll notice that we declare that it extends from something, namely a file called `layout`, and then we specify the page itself in the `content` section. Let's actually create our layout that we'll share between all of our pages in `app/views/layout.blade.php`:

```
<!DOCTYPE html>
<html>
<head>
  <title>Conferences</title>
  <link rel="stylesheet" href="//netdna.bootstrapcdn.com/
  bootstrap/3.1.1/css/bootstrap.min.css">
  <link rel="stylesheet" href="//netdna.bootstrapcdn.com/
  bootstrap/3.1.1/css/bootstrap-theme.min.css">
  <script src="//netdna.bootstrapcdn.com/
  bootstrap/3.1.1/js/bootstrap.min.js"></script>
</head>
<body>
  <div class="container">
    <h1>My Conferences</h1>
    <div class="well well-sm">
      <p>
        {{ link_to_route('conferences.index', "Home", null,
        array('class' => 'btn btn-primary')) }}
        {{ link_to_route('conferences.archived', "Archived", null,
        array('class' => 'btn btn-default')) }}
        {{ link_to_route('conferences.new', "Set up a new
        conference", null, array('class' => 'btn btn-info')) }}
      </p>
    </div>
    @if (Session::has('notice'))
      <div class="alert alert-info">
        {{ Session::get('notice') }}
      </div>
```

```
  @endif
  @if (Session::has('success'))
    <div class="alert alert-success">
      {{ Session::get('success') }}
    </div>
  @endif
  @yield('content')
</div>
<script src="//code.jquery.com/jquery-1.11.0.min.js"></script>
<script src="//code.jquery.com/jquery-migrate-1.2.1.min.js"></script>
</body>
</html>
```

In our layout, we do the following:

1. Open our HTML document as usual, and include some external files, particularly, jQuery and the **Bootstrap** (`http://getbootstrap.com`) frontend framework.

2. Inside the body, we add a few links to pages in order to view and create conferences using the `link_to_route` function.

3. After this, we check whether a notice or success message is supplied in the session, and if it is, we display it in a style alert box. We'll set these from our controller later.

4. Finally, we ask Blade to include the `content` section from the view.

We can now view a list of conferences, but we can't actually create them. Let's make this possible now by adding some more methods to `ConferencesController.php`:

```
public function build()
  {
    return View::make('conferences/new');
  }
public function create()
  {
    $conference = new Conference(Input::get('conference'));
    if (!$conference->save()) {
      return Redirect::route('conferences.new')-
>withErrors($conference->getErrors());
    } else {
      rcturn Redirect::route('conferences.show', array('id' =>
$conference->id))
        ->withSuccess("This conference was created successfully.");
    }
  }
```

In the `build` method, we simply load a view and display it.

In the `create` method, we do much more. We create a new `Conference` object using data in the `conference` parameter that comes in with the request, and then we attempt to save it.

If it gets saved successfully, we redirect to the new conference's page with a success message. If something goes wrong (most likely, the validation failed because a name was not provided), we send the user back to the form, including the error(s) to be displayed.

Now, let's create the `app/views/conferences/new.blade.php` view with a form for creating a new conference:

```
@extends('layout')
@section('content')
  <h2>Set up a new conference</h2>
  <p>Enter details below, and we'll give you phone numbers
  and an access code.</p>
  @if ($errors->has())
    <div class="alert-container">
      <ul>
        @foreach ($errors->all() as $error)
          <li>{{ $error }}</li>
        @endforeach
      </ul>
    </div>
  @endif
  {{ Form::open(array('url' => 'conferences', 'role' => 'form')) }}
    <div class="form-group">
      {{ Form::label('conference[name]', 'Name') }}
      {{ Form::text('conference[name]', null, array('class' =>
      'form-control', 'placeholder' => 'Acme Inc. Meeting')) }}
    </div>
    {{ Form::submit('Create', array('class' => 'btn btn-default
    btn-large btn-block submit'))}}
  {{ Form::close() }}
@stop
```

Here, we loop through and display errors generated from the form, if there are any, and then we construct a `<form>` tag using Laravel's form helpers. You can read more about how they work at `http://laravel.com/docs/4.2/html`.

Provided our submission is successful, the controller will try to redirect us to the conference's individual page, which we haven't created yet. From there, users will be able to view a conference's details and edit it if necessary. Let's make that now. We'll start by adding some more methods to `ConferencesController`:

```
public function show($id)
  {
    $conference = Conference::find($id);
    return View::make('conferences/show', array('conference' =>
    $conference));
  }
public function archive($id)
  {
    $conference = Conference::find($id);
    $conference->active = false;
    if ($conference->save()) {
      return Redirect::route('conferences.show', array('id' =>
      $conference->id))->
        withSuccess("This conference has been archived
        successfully.");
    } else {
      return Redirect::route('conferences.show', array('id' =>
      $conference->id))->
        withErrors($conference->getErrors());
    }
  }
public function unarchive($id)
  {
    $conference = Conference::find($id);
    $conference->active = true;
    if ($conference->save()) {
      return Redirect::route('conferences.show', array('id' =>
      $conference->id))->
        withSuccess("This conference has been unarchived
        successfully.");
    } else {
      return Redirect::route('conferences.show', array('id' =>
      $conference->id))->
        withErrors($conference->getErrors());
    }
  }
public function update($id)
  {
    $conference = Conference::find($id);
    $conference->fill(Input::all());
```

```
    if ($conference->save()) {
      return Redirect::route('conferences.show', array('id' =>
      $conference->id))->
        withSuccess("This conference has been updated successfully.");
    } else {
      return Redirect::route('conferences.show', array('id' =>
      $conference->id))->
        withErrors($conference->getErrors());
    }
  }
}
```

There's a lot going on here. First, you'll notice that all of these methods have an $id argument passed in. We specified this earlier in routes.php with the {id} placeholder.

In the show method, we find the conference by its ID, and then we render a view, passing that conference in.

In the other methods we've just added that manipulate the conference in some way we load the conference, make some changes to it (either by manually changing an attribute or by passing an array of input into the fill method, for example, in the update method), and then attempt to save it. We then redirect with appropriate messages based on whether it was saved successfully.

Let's create our last CRUD view, which is show.blade.php:

```
@extends('layout')
@section('content')
  <h2>{{ $conference->name }}</h2>
  <div class="well">
    @if ($conference->active)
      <p>
        To access this conference, participants should dial
        <your phone number here> and use access code {{
        $conference->access_code }}.
      </p>
      <p>
        {{ Form::open(array('route' =>
        array('conferences.archive', $conference->id), 'method' =>
        'put')) }}
          <button type="submit" class="btn">Archive this
          conference</button>
        {{ Form::close() }}
      </p>
    @else
      <p>This conference is archived, so it isn't open to new
      participants right now.</p>
```

```
    <p>
      {{ Form::open(array('route' =>
      array('conferences.unarchive', $conference->id), 'method'
      => 'put')) }}
        <button type="submit" class="btn">Unarchive this
        conference</button>
      {{ Form::close() }}
    </p>
  @endif
  @if ($conference->recording_url)
    <p>
      <audio controls preload='none'><source src='{{
      $conference->recording_url }}' type='audio/mp3' /></audio>
    </p>
  @else
    <p>Once the call is over, you'll be able to listen to a
    recording by clicking on this call in the "Archived"
    section.</p>
  @endif
</div>
<h3>Edit conference</h3>
{{ Form::model($conference, array('route' =>
array('conferences.update', $conference->id), 'role' => 'form'))
}}
  @if ($errors->has())
    <div class="alert-container">
      <ul>
        @foreach ($errors->all() as $error)
          <li>{{ $error }}</li>
        @endforeach
      </ul>
    </div>
  @endif
  <div class="form-group">
    {{ Form::label('name', 'Name') }}
    {{ Form::text('name') }}
  </div>
  {{ Form::submit('Save', array('class' => 'btn btn-default btn-
  large btn-block submit')) }}
{{ Form::close() }}
@stop
```

Let's go through this and discuss what we're doing in this view:

1. First, we display the conference's name.

2. Next, we modify what we show based on whether the conference is active or archived, choosing whether or not to display dial-in details. We're also adding an **Archive this conference** and **Unarchive this conference** button as appropriate, making a PUT request from it to the relevant action. Make sure you fill in one of your Twilio phone numbers here at the *highlighted* point in the code.

3. If the conference has a recording URL recorded, we display an <audio> tag, playing our recording back.

4. Finally, we have a form for updating the Conference object, which is built using not Form::open but Form::model and pointing to our update action. Using Form::model means that the form fields will automatically display the current value stored in the database (for example, the conference's name in the name field).

Handling inbound calls

We've now built a full CRUD interface where we can create, view, and update our conferences, ultimately getting the phone number and access code. Let's actually link all this up to Twilio.

First, add the following to app/routes.php. We specify two methods on a new TwilioController, plus new actions to go with individual calls referred to by their $id:

```
Route::get('/twilio', array(
   'as' => 'twilio.index',
   'uses' => 'TwilioController@index'
));
Route::post('/twilio/access_code', array(
   'as' => 'twilio.access_code',
   'uses' => 'TwilioController@access_code'
));
Route::get('/conferences/{id}/twiml', array(
   'as' => 'conferences.twiml',
   'uses' => 'ConferencesController@twiml'
));
Route::post('/conferences/{id}/callback', array(
   'as' => 'conferences.callback',
   'uses' => 'ConferencesController@callback'
));
```

Now, let's create app/controllers/TwilioController.php, putting the following into it:

```php
<?php
class TwilioController extends BaseController {
  public function index()
  {
    $view = View::make('twilio/index');
    $response = Response::make($view, 200);
    $response->header('Content-Type', 'application/xml');
    return $response;
  }
  public function access_code()
  {
    $conference = Conference::active()->where('access_code', '=',
Input::get('Digits'))->first();
    if ($conference) {
      return Redirect::route('conferences.twiml', array('id' =>
$conference->id));
    } else {
      $view = View::make('twilio/access_code');
      $response = Response::make($view, 200);
      $response->header('Content-Type', 'application/xml');
      return $view;
    }
  }
}
```

In the index method, we load a view and display it, manually setting headers to specify that this is an XML file.

In the access_code method, we use the user's keypad input provided in the Digits parameter to look for active conferences that match the provided access code. If an active conference is found, we redirect to its TwiML, and if not, we display a view.

Let's create our two very simple and static TwiML XML views, starting with index. blade.php, which you should put in app/views/twilio:

```xml
<?xml version="1.0" encoding="UTF-8"?>
<Response>
  <Gather timeout="20" numDigits="6" method="POST"
  action="/twilio/access_code">
    <Play>http://assets.twiliobestpractices.com/conferences/
    index.mp3</Play>
  </Gather>
</Response>
```

This plays a welcome message to the caller and collects six digits of input, posting them to our `access_code` method when done. Now, let's create `access_code.blade.php`:

```xml
<?xml version="1.0" encoding="UTF-8"?>
<Response>
    <Play>http://assets.twiliobestpractices.com/conferences/
    access_code.mp3</Play>
    <Redirect method="GET">/twilio</Redirect>
</Response>
```

This piece of TwiML is even simpler, playing an error message and then redirecting back to the first piece of TwiML to ask for the access code again.

In our controller's `access_code` method, if we successfully find a conference by its access code, we redirect to the `ConferenceController@twiml` controller action. Let's get this set up now.

In `ConferenceController`, add the following. As you'll recognize, this is some very standard Laravel PHP that loads the conference by its provided ID and then builds and renders a view using it:

```php
public function twiml($id)
    {
        $conference = Conference::find($id);
        $view = View::make('conferences/twiml', array('conference' =>
        $conference));
        $response = Response::make($view, 200);
        $response->header('Content-Type', 'application/xml');
        return $response;
    }
```

To go alongside that, let's create a new view for the TwiML at `app/views/conferences/twiml.blade.php`:

```xml
<?xml version="1.0" encoding="UTF-8"?>
<Response>
    <Play>http://assets.twiliobestpractices.com/
    conferences/show.mp3</Play>
    <Dial>
        <Conference beep="true" record="record-from-start"
        eventCallbackUrl="/conferences/{{{ $conference->
        id }}}/callback">
            {{{ $conference->access_code }}}
        </Conference>
    </Dial>
</Response>
```

Our TwiML plays a short welcome message to the caller before dialing through to the conference. We ask Twilio to record the call from the start, and we also ask it to beep when new people join and to ping a callback URL for the conference when something interesting happens.

Finally, inside the `<Conference>` noun, we specify our access code as the name of the conference room.

Now that everything's set up, we'll need to actually link this to a Twilio number. To do this, set up a phone number to request `/twilio` when there's an incoming call. See *Chapter 1, Working with TwiML*, for instructions on how to do this.

 You can still use ngrok with the Laravel Homestead web server on port `8000` to make your code accessible to Twilio from the Internet.

Archiving conferences and storing recordings

We're nearly there. We can now create a conference from the web interface and have callers dial in with their access code.

The last piece in the puzzle is to be able to archive a conference and store its recording automatically when it finishes. To do this, let's set up `ConferencesController@callback`, adding the following method to the controller:

```
public function callback($id)
  {
    $conference = Conference::find($id);
    $conference->recording_url = Input::get('RecordingUrl');
    $conference->active = false;
    $conference->save();
    return Response::make("Success", 200);
  }
```

In `twiml.blade.php` earlier, we asked Twilio to ping this route when an event occurred on our conference.

In particular, we are notified when the conference finishes, that is, when all participants have left. In this controller action, we load the conference by its ID, set the recording URL to the one Twilio provides, archive the conference, and then save it before responding with a `200` response.

The conference will move to the **Archived** page in our interface and will include an audio player to listen to the recording on its page.

And you're done!

You've now built a fully featured conferencing tool. You've not only gotten to grips with Twilio, but also learned how to improve the structure of your applications using Laravel, which is an MVC framework.

Here are some ideas for further enhancements:

- Require a login to access the CRUD interface. You can do this using Laravel's built-in authentication (`http://laravel.com/docs/4.2/security`).

- Allow callers to dial in using their browser with Twilio Client. Head back to *Chapter 3, Calling in the Browser with Twilio Client* for help on doing this.

Summary

In this chapter, we learned a lot by building two exciting projects.

First, we built a callback request application where we made outgoing calls using the Twilio REST API and used `StatusCallback` to check up on the status of calls.

Secondly, we created a more advanced app: a conference calling system. Here we learned to structure our applications in a maintainable way using Laravel and worked with Twilio's conferencing functionality.

So far, we've stuck almost entirely to Twilio's PHP library. In the next chapter, we'll briefly learn how to get started, work with, and learn more about the libraries Twilio offers for other languages, such as Ruby, Java, and .NET.

5
Twilio in your language

In this chapter, we'll get to grips with working with Twilio in languages other than PHP, looking at all six of the remaining API libraries:

- Ruby
- Python
- C#
- Java
- Node
- Apex (Salesforce's proprietary language)

For each library, we'll learn how to install it, how to instantiate the REST API client, and will briefly see how the syntax of its calls compare with the PHP library we've used throughout the book. We'll also have a quick recap of the PHP library for ease of comparison.

All of the code samples are named, and can be found in the code samples downloadable from Packt's website.

As a general rule, it's bad practice to include your account SID and auth token in your code for security reasons. These should be set in TWILIO_ACCOUNT_SID and TWILIO_AUTH_TOKEN environment variables and then used in your code.

You can find helpful examples on setting environment variables in different platforms at https://github.com/twilio/starter-ruby/blob/bc41654418c21576f63d95e15cb96c744e555fff/README.md#setting-up.

PHP – a recap

We've already worked with the PHP library in *Chapter 2, Exploring the REST API*, but it's worth a quick recap so we can see more clearly how it compares with libraries in the other languages we'll be looking at.

To get a hold of the PHP library, we *can* manually download its source and include it into our project ourselves. However, it's much better to use Composer, which is a dependency management tool for PHP.

First, you'll need to install Composer for your platform. Follow the instructions at https://getcomposer.org/doc/00-intro.md to get up and running.

Once Composer is set up, simply run this in your project directory:

```
composer require twilio/sdk dev-master
```

This will create a composer.json file for you to record your and then will add the Twilio library to this file, download the library and all of its dependencies, and generate an autoload.php file.

Now that the library is installed into our project, we can set up the client as follows:

```php
<?php
// Require Composer's autoload file, bringing in the Twilio library
require('vendor/autoload.php');
$accountSid = $_ENV["TWILIO_ACCOUNT_SID"];
$authToken = $_ENV["TWILIO_AUTH_TOKEN"];
$client = new Services_Twilio($accountSid, $authToken);
?>
```

Now that we've instantiated the API client, we can send an SMS like this:

```php
$message = $client->account->messages->sendMessage("+441290211998",
"+441290211999", "This is a message from the first number, to the
second, with this in the body.");
```

 For a wealth of other examples from the PHP library, head back to *Chapter 2, Exploring the REST API*, or refer to the official library documentation at https://twilio-php. readthedocs.org/en/latest/.

Ruby

We can install the `twilio-ruby` library using the ubiquitous **RubyGems** software. Much like Composer in the PHP world, it's a package manager that makes it easy to install and manage dependencies.

We can install the gem on its own by running `gem install twilio-ruby` from a terminal/Command Prompt. This will make the gem available in **Interactive Ruby Shell (IRB)**.

However, in the context of a Ruby project, we usually manage our gem dependencies through a `Gemfile`. This file specifies a source for downloading gems, usually `https://rubygems.org`, and then lists gems to be installed. You also have the ability to specify the version you want to use and can install different sets of gems for different environments (for instance, you might have different gems for production use and running tests).

A basic `Gemfile` using the Twilio library would look like this:

```
source "https://rubygems.org"
gem 'twilio-ruby', '~> 3.12'
```

Once we've added the gem to our dependencies, we can install the library with **Bundler**. Most likely, you already have Bundler installed. You can ensure that this is the case by running `gem install bundler` — and then, just run `bundle install` from your project directory. It'll install `twilio-ruby` plus its dependencies and their dependencies, and so on.

> If you're like me, you'll often want to play with the API from the command line. You can do this by installing the `twilio-ruby` gem outside of a `Gemfile` and then running `irb` plus the `require 'twilio-ruby'` command once you're in `irb`.

In our individual code files, we'll just need to include `require 'twilio-ruby'` in order to make the library available. We're now ready to set up the client with our account SID and auth token.

We have two options. First we can instantiate an individual client (`individual_client.rb`) like this:

```
require 'twilio-ruby'
account_sid = ENV['TWILIO_ACCOUNT_SID']
auth_token = ENV['TWILIO_AUTH_TOKEN']
client = Twilio::REST::Client.new account_sid, auth_token
```

Alternatively, as of the most recent versions of the Ruby library, we can set the configuration once, and then use it automatically later. This would be the normal approach if you're working with a Ruby framework, such as Ruby on Rails (http://rubyonrails.org).

We can instantiate a shared client (shared_client.rb) like this:

```
require 'twilio-ruby'
account_sid = ENV['TWILIO_ACCOUNT_SID']
auth_token = ENV['TWILIO_AUTH_TOKEN']
Twilio.configure do |config|
  config.account_sid = account_sid
  config.auth_token = auth_token
end
# and then, anywhere we want to use the client...
client = Twilio::REST::Client.new
```

Once we've instantiated a client, we can make API calls using it (send_sms.rb):

```
message = client.messages.create(
  from: '+441290211999',
  to: '+441708300116',
  body: 'This is an SMS message.'
)
```

If you look back to the PHP examples we saw earlier, you'll see that the syntax here is very comparable to PHP. The main difference is that in the Ruby library, we'll tend to pass hashes (known in other languages, such as Python, as dictionaries) of arguments by name, making our code easier to read.

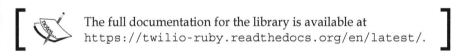

The full documentation for the library is available at https://twilio-ruby.readthedocs.org/en/latest/.

Python

We can install the Twilio package for Python using **pip**, which is Python's standard package manager.

If you don't have pip installed, follow the instructions at https://pip.pypa.io/en/latest/installing.html to install it.

To install the package, simply run the `pip install twilio` command.

In your code, you'll just need to import the library, and then you can instantiate the client (`client.py`) like this:

```
from twilio.rest import TwilioRestClient
import os
account_sid = os.environ.get('TWILIO_ACCOUNT_SID')
auth_token = os.environ.get('TWILIO_AUTH_TOKEN')
client = TwilioRestClient(account_sid, auth_token)
```

Once you've set up your client, the syntax for sending an SMS is very similar to the one used in other examples, somewhere between the PHP and Ruby implementation, making use of keyword arguments (`send_sms.py`):

```
message = client.messages.create(to="+441290211999",
from_="+441708300116", body="This is an SMS message.")
```

Here, our `from_` parameter includes an underscore at the end because `from` is a reserved keyword in Python.

 The full documentation is available online at `http://readthedocs.org/docs/twilio-python/en/latest/`.

C#

The C# Twilio library is available on **NuGet** (`https://www.nuget.org`), which is the standard package manager for the Microsoft .NET platform. If you don't have it installed, check out `http://docs.nuget.org/docs/start-here/installing-nuget` for instructions.

To install the package in Visual Studio from within your project, right-click on **References** in your project, choose the **Manage NuGet Packages** option (shown in the following screenshot), and then search for `Twilio`. Find the **Twilio** package, and then click on **Install**.

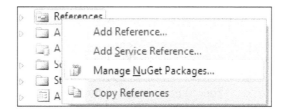

In your code, you'll just need to import the library and then instantiate a client (`client.cs`):

```
using Twilio;
var accountSid = System.Environment.GetEnvironmentVariable("TWILIO_
ACCOUNT_SID")
var authToken = System.Environment.GetEnvironmentVariable("TWILIO_
AUTH_TOKEN")
var client = new TwilioRestClient(accountSid, authToken);
```

Once you've set up your client, the syntax for sending a message is comparable to PHP with pre-determined argument lists (`send_sms.cs`):

```
var message = client.SendMessage("+441290211999", "+441708300116",
"This is an SMS message.");
```

 Extensive documentation on the library and its methods is available at `https://github.com/twilio/twilio-csharp/wiki/Twilio.Api`.

Java

The Twilio Java library can be installed using **Maven** (`http://maven.apache.org/download.cgi`), which is Java's package manager. Installation instructions are available at the aforementioned link if you don't have it installed.

To install the package, add it to the `pom.xml` file in your project's root directory like this:

```
<dependency>
    <groupId>com.twilio.sdk</groupId>
    <artifactId>twilio-java-sdk</artifactId>
    <version>3.4.6</version>
    <scope>compile</scope>
</dependency>
```

Next, run `mvn install` to get Maven to install our new package.

In your code, you'll need to import lots of libraries:

```
import com.twilio.sdk.TwilioRestClient;
import com.twilio.sdk.TwilioRestException;
import com.twilio.sdk.resource.factory.MessageFactory;
import com.twilio.sdk.resource.instance.Message;
import org.apache.http.NameValuePair;
```

```java
import org.apache.http.message.BasicNameValuePair;
import java.util.ArrayList;
import java.util.List;
```

Next, instantiate the library with your account SID and auth token at a relevant place in your code (client.java):

```java
final String accountSid = System.getenv("TWILIO_ACCOUNT_SID");
final String authToken = System.getenv("TWILIO_AUTH_TOKEN");
final TwilioRestClient client = new TwilioRestClient(accountSid,
authToken);
```

Once you've set up your client, the syntax for sending a message is somewhat longer and more verbose than in other languages. Key-value pairs are specified as arguments by adding them to a parameters object (send_sms.java):

```java
final Account mainAccount = client.getAccount();
final MessageFactory messageFactory = mainAccount.getMessageFactory();
final List<NameValuePair> messageParams = new
List<BasicNameValuePair>();
messageParams.add(new BasicNameValuePair("To", "+441708300116"));
messageParams.add(new BasicNameValuePair("From", "+441290211999"));
messageParams.add(new BasicNameValuePair("Body", "This is an SMS
message."));
final Message message = messageFactory.create(messageParams);
```

> The full documentation is available online at
> http://twilio.github.io/twilio-java/.

Node.js

The twilio-node library is available on **npm**, which is Node's package manager that is included when you download Node itself.

To install the library, run npm install twilio --save in your project directory, or npm install -g twilio to install it globally across your machine.

In your code, you'll just need to require the library and instantiate a client (client.js):

```javascript
var account_sid = process.env.TWILIO_ACCOUNT_SID;
var auth_token = process.env.TWILIO_AUTH_TOKEN;
var client = require('twilio')(account_sid, auth_token);
```

The syntax for sending an SMS from this point onwards is similar to Ruby, using a dictionary of arguments.

However, there is a complication in that Node uses **asynchronous** requests when contacting the API, meaning that we can't simply save what the method returns to a variable. Instead, we provide a callback that will be invoked with the Message object once it has been sent successfully (send_sms.js):

```
client.messages.create({
    body: "This is an SMS message.",
    to: "+441708300116",
    from: "+441290211999"
}, function(err, message) {
    process.stdout.write(message.sid);
});
```

 The full documentation for working with Twilio in Node.js is available at http://twilio.github.io/twilio-node/.

Apex for Salesforce.com

Installing the Twilio library for Salesforce's Apex programming language is a little different.

To add the library to your installation, go to https://login.salesforce.com/packaging/installPackage.apexp?p0=04ti0000000XkE0, click on **Continue**, and then follow the instructions.

In your code, you'll then just need to create a client object (client.cls):

```
String accountSid = 'ACXXXXXXXXXXXXXXXXXX';
String authToken = 'YYYYYYYYYYYYYYYYYY';

TwilioRestClient client = new TwilioRestClient(accountSid,
authToken);
```

 The Salesforce platform doesn't have support for environment variables, so we're just going to store them in the code, unlike other examples.

To send an SMS, much like with the Ruby and Python libraries, we pass in a hash (or in Apex, a `Map`) of arguments (`send_sms.cls`), like this:

```
Map<String,String> params = new Map<String,String> {
  'To'   => '+441708300116',
  'From' => '+441290211999',
  'Body' => 'This is an SMS message.'
};
TwilioSMS message =
client.getAccount().getSMSMessages().create(params);
```

 The full documentation for Twilio's Salesforce library is available at `http://twilio-salesforce.readthedocs.org/en/latest/index.html`.

Summary

In this chapter, we looked at all of Twilio's API libraries, learning how to install them and set them up, and comparing their syntax with one another as well as with the PHP library we've used in previous chapters.

In the next chapter, we'll learn how to keep our Twilio account and applications secure using features such as two-factor authentication.

6
Securing your Twilio App

In this chapter, we'll learn how to keep our Twilio account and applications (and ultimately credit) secure by:

- Enabling two-factor authentication on our Twilio account
- Verifying that requests to our application are really coming from Twilio
- Setting up a circuit breaker for our account and any subaccounts

Enabling two-factor authentication

Twilio offers **two-factor authentication** functionality that we can enable on our account.

This will give you much greater security if someone tries to break into your account following the *something you know and something you have* model. Apart from your password, Twilio will send you an SMS or call you when a login attempt is made, requiring you to enter a one-time password.

Not only will this largely prevent malicious access to your account, but you'll also know that someone is attempting to access your account, and what's more, that they have your password.

 It's worth noting that, unsurprisingly, you can quite easily roll two-factor authentication functionality for your own application using Twilio's call and SMS functionality. Check out https://www.twilio.com/docs/howto/two-factor-authentication for help with getting started.

There are two steps to enable two-factor authentication:

1. First, you'll need to add a phone number. You can do this from your Twilio dashboard by clicking on the dropdown in the top-right corner, and then clicking on the first entry with your name and e-mail address.

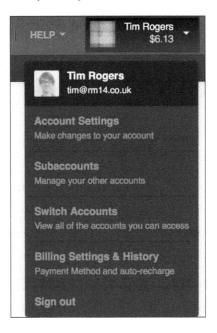

2. Next, click on **Add phone number**, and then enter your phone number. Twilio will send you an SMS (or alternatively, call you if you'd like), thereby ensuring that you own the phone number that you've provided.

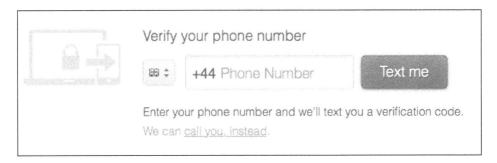

Once you've added and verified your phone number on your user profile, you'll need to set up two-factor authentication on your account(s). To get to the right place, click on **Account Settings** in the dropdown.

 If your login has been given access to another user's Twilio account, (that is, the account you access from the **Switch Accounts** menu option) an administrator on that account will need to repeat this process.

From this page, you'll be able to choose between two different two-factor options (you can also disable the feature here):

- **Once Per Computer**: This will effectively make the device you're using trusted, which means that subsequent logins for the next 30 days won't require you to use your phone.
- **Every log-in**: Every time you try to log in to Twilio, you'll have to provide a one-time password from your phone.

Once you're done, click on the **Save Settings** button at the bottom of your page to set up the two-factor authentication.

 There are a couple of other features you might want to check out on the **Account Settings** page.

You can reset your API credentials if you accidentally reveal them and you can disable parts of Twilio's Request Inspector which might potentially store sensitive information from your application and require passwords in order to access recordings and media you send in MMS messages.

Verifying that requests are from Twilio

If parties other than Twilio are able to make requests to your application, they can potentially change and corrupt data or access sensitive information.

Without authentication measures, if an attacker was able to guess the URLs of the endpoints on your application that Twilio hits with its webhooks, they could wreak havoc. For instance, they could spoof fake SMS messages so that they appear to come from users or they could access the private phones numbers of users they should only be able to call through a public line you provide.

There are two routes you can take to prevent this, ensuring with a reasonable degree of certainty that a request genuinely comes from Twilio:

- Set up HTTP Basic Authentication
- Verify the signature of requests to ensure they're signed by Twilio

HTTP Basic Authentication

HTTP Basic Authentication simply allows you to require a username and password to access your web server's resources.

If you're working with PHP, you'll want to set this up on the web server level. This is possible in most servers, including:

- Apache (`http://httpd.apache.org/docs/2.2/howto/auth.html#gettingitworking`)
- Nginx (`https://www.digitalocean.com/community/tutorials/how-to-set-up-http-authentication-with-nginx-on-ubuntu-12-10`)
- IIS (`http://technet.microsoft.com/en-us/library/cc772009(v=ws.10).aspx`)

If you're not using one of these, you can be virtually certain anyway that this option will be available to you; simply have a look at its documentation or search the web.

Alternatively, you can implement Basic Authentication in your PHP code using code along these lines (`http_basic.php` in this chapter's code samples). We'll store the username and password in environment variables for security (see *Chapter 2, Exploring the REST API*, for details):

```php
<?php
if (!isset($_SERVER['PHP_AUTH_USER'])) {
  // The user didn't even try to authenticate, so sent 401
Unauthorized
  header('WWW-Authenticate: Basic realm="Twilio only!"');
```

```
  header('HTTP/1.0 401 Unauthorized');
  exit;
} elseif ($_SERVER['PHP_AUTH_USER'] == $_ENV["TWILIO_USERNAME"] && $_
SERVER['PHP_AUTH_PW'] == $_ENV["TWILIO_PASSWORD"]) {
  // The user authenticated successfully, so perform actions and
output TwiML
} else {
  // The user tried to authenticate, but didn't have the right
credentials
  header('WWW-Authenticate: Basic realm="Twilio only!"');
  header('HTTP/1.0 401 Unauthorized');
  exit;
}
?>
```

Let's go through this bit by bit:

- If `$_SERVER['PHP_AUTH_USER']` isn't set, then no username and password has been provided, so we respond with a `401 Unauthorized` error (that is, a header request, and the user provides a username and password, as well as the `WWW-Authenticate` header), which will make browsers display **Twilio only!** in the login dialog.

- If the provided username and password do match what is stored in the `TWILIO_USERNAME` and `TWILIO_PASSWORD` environment variables respectively, then we perform actions that the request requires and respond with TwiML.

- If a username and password was provided, but didn't match those we expected, then we send our `401` error and associated headers again.

When we're providing a URL to Twilio (for instance, when initiating a call via the REST API, or setting it for incoming calls or SMS messages from our Dashboard), we can set the username and password in this format:

```
https://twilio:secretpassword@www.myserver.com/my_secure_document
```

Verifying the signature

Alternatively, instead of using a username and password, we can verify the cryptographic signature Twilio generates with its requests based upon our auth token which is sent in the X-Twilio-Signature header.

The scheme for doing this is somewhat complicated (you can find it in full at https://www.twilio.com/docs/security#validating-requests) but fortunately, Twilio provides validation functionality in their API libraries alongside code samples.

For this method of verification to be available, you'll need to serve your application over HTTPS with **Transport Layer Security** (**TLS**) enabled. In fact, you should *always* do this with your Twilio application, as a good security practice.

 Following the SSLv3 vulnerability discovered in October, 2014 known as POODLE, you'll want to double-check the security of any SSL configuration. See https://www.digitalocean.com/community/tutorials/how-to-protect-your-server-against-the-poodle-sslv3-vulnerability for details.

In PHP, we'd execute the following (see the signature.php file in the code samples):

```php
<?php
// Load auth token from the TWILIO_AUTH_TOKEN environment variable
$authToken = $_ENV['TWILIO_AUTH_TOKEN'];
// You'll need to make sure the Twilio library is included, either by requiring
// it manually or loading Composer's autoload.php
$validator = new Services_Twilio_RequestValidator($authToken);
$url = $_SERVER["SCRIPT_URI"];
$vars = $_GET;
$signature = $_SERVER["HTTP_X_TWILIO_SIGNATURE"];
if ($validator->validate($signature, $url, $vars)) {
  // This request definitely came from Twilio, so continue onwards...
} else {
  // Watch out - this is not a real request from Twilio.
header('HTTP/1.0 401 Unauthorized');
}
?>
```

Here, we instantiate a `Services_Twilio_RequestValidator` object from the API library with our auth token before passing in the requested URL, the request body (`$_GET` in this case, but for a `POST` request, this would be `$_POST`), and the signature.

We then call the validator's `validate` method with these pieces of data, allowing it to generate the signature itself, and comparing it against what we received in the `X-Twilio-Signature` header. If it matches, the request is genuine, but if not, the request is spoofed and is not from Twilio.

Building a circuit breaker

Using Twilio's Usage Triggers, which we saw in *Chapter 2*, *Exploring the REST API*, allows us to build a circuit breaker.

In short, this will let us know when one of our subaccounts passes certain amounts of usage, which will help us detect possible abuse of our account, as well as mistakes in our code. It can even help detect abuse if we were running a multitenant app (that is, offering Twilio-based services to our users).

When our specified usage threshold is surpassed, Twilio will send a webhook to a URL of our choice. From this URL, we can perform a range of actions, whether that is sending ourselves an e-mail or even suspending the account in question.

For more details on Usage Triggers and how to specify them, head back to *Chapter 2*, *Exploring the REST API*. Here, we'll just run through a quick example of suspending an account if it spends more than $50 in one day.

We'll set up our Usage Trigger using the Twilio dashboard. To do this, first log in, and then switch to the appropriate subaccount you'd like to set up the trigger for by clicking on your name in the top-right corner. Next, click on **Subaccounts**, and then click on the desired account.

Next, click on **Usage** in the navigation bar, then click on **Triggers** underneath, and then click on the **Create Usage Trigger** button.

Fill out the fields as shown in the following image. First, you'll need to click on the **Trigger a webhook** link on the right-hand side of the page where **Send an email** appears in the screenshot to set up a webhook, replacing the URL with one that would be accessible from a domain of your own, of course.

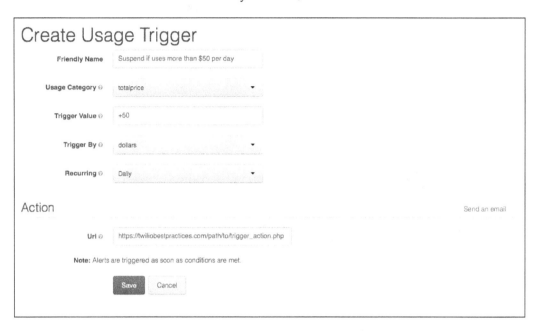

We might also want to automate this process of setting up a usage trigger using the REST API. For example, we might want to automatically suspend a subaccount we've just created for a customer if their usage goes beyond reasonable limits. In order to do so, we'd do the same thing we did previously in PHP like this:

```php
<?php
$accountSid = $_ENV['TWILIO_ACCOUNT_SID'];
$authToken = $_ENV['TWILIO_AUTH_TOKEN'];
$subaccountSid = '<the SID of the subaccount>';
// You'll need to make sure the Twilio library is included,
either by requiring
// it manually or loading Composer's autoload.php
$client = new Services_Twilio($accountSid, $authToken);
$account = $client->accounts->get($subaccountSid);
$account->usage_triggers->create(
  'totalprice',
  '+50',
  'https://twiliobestpractices.com/path/to/trigger_action.php',
  array(
    'Recurring' => 'daily',
```

```
        'TriggerBy' => 'price',
        'FriendlyName' => 'Suspend if uses more than $50 per day'
    )
);
?>
```

Both options do exactly the same thing. They create a trigger that will send a webhook to `https://twiliobestpractices.com/path/to/trigger_action.php` when more than $50 is spent by our subaccount on any one day.

It's completely up to us what we do from the endpoint that receives the webhook. Anything we can program is possible, from suspending the account to calling an engineer to look into it.

Here's some example code (`trigger_action.php`) to go with the usage trigger we just set up that will automatically suspend the account once it goes over $50 spend in a day.

In this code sample, we also verify the authenticity of the request, as we saw previously, making sure that this is a genuine Usage Trigger webhook from Twilio:

```
<?php
// Before starting, you'll need to require the Twilio PHP library
// We'll load the SID of the subaccount that the trigger relates to and its
// auth token from environment variables, but in reality, you're likely to be
// loading them from a database of your users' details based on a passed-in ID,
// or something along those lines.
$subaccountSid = $_ENV['TWILIO_SUBACCOUNT_SID'];
$subaccountAuthToken = $_ENV['TWILIO_SUBACCOUNT_AUTH_TOKEN'];
$url = $_SERVER['SCRIPT_URI'];
$signature = $_SERVER['HTTP_X_TWILIO_SIGNATURE'];
$validator = new Services_Twilio_RequestValidator($subaccountAuthToken);
if ($validator->validate($signature, $url, $_POST)) {
    $client = new Services_Twilio($subaccountSid, $subaccountAuthToken);
    $client->account->update(array('Status' => 'suspended'));
} else {
    header('HTTP/1.0 401 Unauthorized');
}
?>
```

We've shown you examples of doing all of this using the PHP library, but you can do it with any of Twilio's libraries . You can also do this directly with the REST API using a tool such as Postman. See *Chapter 5, Twilio in your language*, for details.

Summary

In this chapter, we covered three helpful tips to keep your Twilio account and application secure:

- First, we enabled Two-Factor Authentication to keep our account secure, even if someone finds out our password.

- Next, we learned how to make sure that the requests your app receives genuinely come from Twilio, by either using the HTTP Basic Authentication or by verifying the cryptographic request signature.

- Finally, we set up alerts to inform us and take appropriate action when certain usage thresholds are reached using Twilio's Usage Triggers, helping protect your app from abuse and coding errors.

In the next chapter, we'll learn how to effectively test and debug our applications and make them ready for release.

7
Testing, Debugging, and Deploying Twilio Apps

In this chapter, we'll learn how to test, debug, and monitor the Twilio applications we've built, making sure that they're ready for production. Specifically, we'll discover how to:

- Make sure we try out every part of the application flow by drawing and following a flowchart
- Use the App Monitor to watch for errors in our implementation
- Wield the Request Inspector to track down and fix errors
- Fix some of the most common errors

The power of flowcharts

As developers, we can often be somewhat disparaging about things we see as low tech, such as putting together detailed plans for what we're building! However, when we're building a complex Twilio application, creating a flowchart at the beginning of a project is invaluable when it comes to not only implementing, but also testing what we've built.

In order to properly test an application, you need to follow every branch in its application flow and check whether it behaves as expected. The best way to do this is to define your expectations upfront before you even start writing code.

A great way to do this is to draw a **flowchart**. A flowchart represents a flow in our application, including any decisions that need to be made—effectively creating branches—and the outcomes from these decisions.

We can either build these on paper, or use a range of great online tools. I use Draw.io (`http://draw.io`), but plenty of other great options are only a Google search away. I've included some others in *Chapter 8, Online Resources*.

As an example, let's think back to the conference calling app that we built in *Chapter 4, Twilio in the Real World*. Here's a simple flowchart that represents this application:

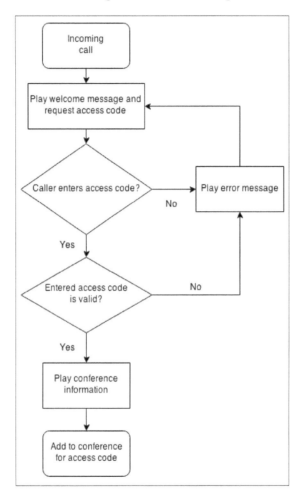

As you'll see, our flowchart clearly explains what happens from a caller dialing in to them getting added to a Twilio conference room and them being ready to chat with other participants:

- The rounded rectangles, such as the one at the top that reads **Incoming call**, represent entry and exit points of our flow — at the start, a caller dials in, and at the end, they're placed in a conference.

- The rectangles represent generic parts of the flow. Here, some kind of action is performed, such as playing a message, in our case.

- The rhombuses (*diamonds*) represent decisions. Coming from the diamonds, you'll see two arrows labeled **Yes** and **No**. For example, we can use these to model different options in a phone menu (for example, pressing 1 or 2).

  Depending on the answer to the question, the caller is taken down one of two (or more) routes. For example, if they enter in an access code that exists, they hear the conference welcome message, and if not, they hear an error and are asked to try again.

Our flowchart helps us test our application because it gives us really clear visibility as to what should happen.

Before we deploy our application into production—and indeed, as we build it—we should follow through this flow, making calls to our application (or sending SMSes or going through any other appropriate flows), following every possible decision and checking whether what we expect actually happens.

To use the conference calling application as an example, we'd call in multiple times, trying all of the possible combinations. For one call, we'd enter no access code and check whether we hear the error, then we'd enter a nonexistent access code and listen for the error, and finally, we'd enter a real access code and check whether we're joined to the conference.

A word on automated testing

Especially when your application gets bigger, you're best off moving away from manual testing toward automated testing. Following an automated testing process, you essentially write code that tests your code, going through all of the different processes and checking whether the results are correct automatically.

For example, our tests would request the incoming call TwiML and check whether it contained what we expected (a `<Play>` verb with a welcome message inside a `<Gather>` verb). It would then try requesting `/twilio/access_code` with no access code, and then an invalid access code, and so on. This process can be automatically run in seconds with no human intervention.

Help with automated testing is out of the scope of this book, but testing frameworks are available in most languages, including PHP. You'll find links in the next chapter.

Using the App Monitor

When we're using the REST API, Twilio simply returns any errors to us in the response, which are then usually flagged up by the library we're using. Things aren't quite as simple when it comes to errors that occur when Twilio makes a request to us.

Twilio's **App Monitor** automatically monitors and records errors in our applications. This means that we should be able to easily detect any errors we don't pick up when testing ourselves before we deploy our app.

The App Monitor, which is located under **Dev tools** in the Twilio dashboard (shown below), lists error codes that have occurred alongside the number of times they've been seen in your application and the time when the error last occurred.

To access the App Monitor, click on **Dev Tools** in the dashboard navigation bar, and then click on **App Monitor**.

Click on an error in the list to get more details. You'll see data on how often the error has occurred (including a helpful graph), a useful description of what the error means, and a **Request Inspector** with all of the requests where the error has occurred.

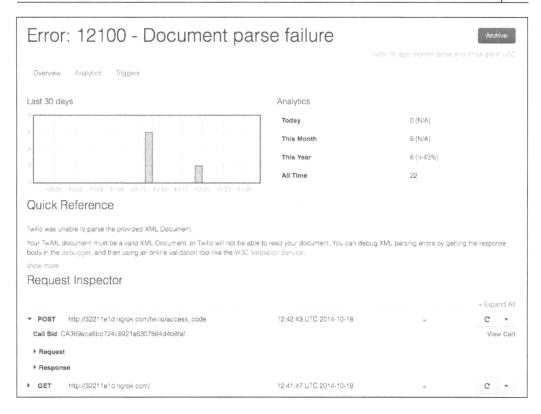

The App Monitor not only helps us keep track of errors that have occurred in our app, but it also gives us the information we need to be able to fix them. It also helps us test our fix. At the heart of this power is the Request Inspector; we'll look at how to use it next.

Once you've fixed an error, click on the **Archive** button to the top-right of the error's page, or put a tick on it in the list of errors on the **App Monitor** page, and then click on **Archive Selected**.

Archiving our errors will help us keep track of when we think we've fixed them and will allow us to return later if we see a regression, that is, if the error comes back.

Using Triggers in the App Monitor

The App Monitor allows us to set up triggers when certain kinds of error occur. This way, Twilio will drop an e-mail to us, allowing us to take urgent action. To set up a trigger:

1. Click on **Triggers** on the **App Monitor** page:

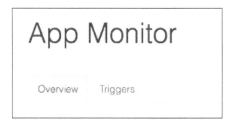

2. Next, click on the **Create New Trigger** button in the top-right corner. Now, we'll specify the details for our trigger and the kind of errors that should cause us to receive an e-mail.

   As an example, we might want to be alerted if our server goes down. When this happens, Twilio's `11205 - HTTP connection failure` error is triggered:

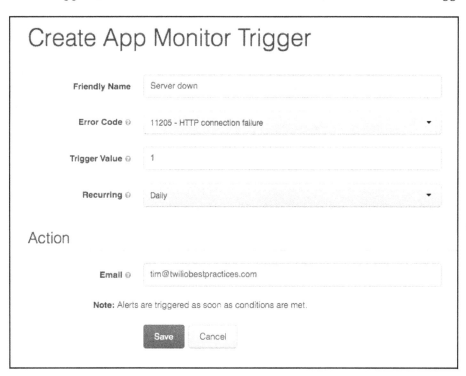

We give our trigger a friendly name, and then specify the error we want to watch out for. We can even set this to monitor *any* errors. Next, we specify a trigger value of 1 and set our trigger to run daily. This means that our trigger will be fired if there is ever more than one of these errors in a day.

3. Finally, we specify the e-mail to be notified when our trigger fires and click on **Save**.

 By clicking on the **Trigger a webhook** link to the right of the e-mail field, we can receive a webhook when our trigger fires instead. With this, we can take an alternative automatic action, for example, sending one of our developers an SMS (using Twilio, naturally).

Using the Request Inspector

Alongside our errors in the App Monitor, there is a Request Inspector that let us see the requests that triggered the recorded error.

This Request Inspector is also used elsewhere: for instance, when we view the logs for a particular call or SMS from the **Logs** page in the navigation bar, we'll also have access to this powerful tool.

The Request Inspector is a relatively new and late addition to Twilio, but is one that makes debugging our applications so much easier by letting us not only view all of the details of requests Twilio made to our application, but also letting us retry them in one click.

 All of the data in the Request Inspector is also accessible via the Notifications API; refer to Twilio's documentation at `https://www.twilio.com/docs/api/rest/notification` for details.

At first, Twilio shows you the HTTP method used for the request, the URL that was requested, the time of the request, and the HTTP status that came back:

However, we can expand this to show much more. Simply click on the arrow to the left of the HTTP method, and you'll then see the call or message's SID, plus you can further expand the details to see the request and response, including their headers and contents. In short, we can see exactly what Twilio sent to our application and exactly what came back.

With these details, we'll often be able to identify what caused the error and fix it. For instance, we might see in the expanded **Response Body** that an error was triggered because no digits were entered when we expected them to be entered. Using this information, we'd be able to fix the error for the future.

In many cases, we'll be able to quickly and simply test whether our fix has worked using the retry button on the right-hand side of the inspector. Simply click on that, and Twilio will make the exact same request again and record the response for you. With any luck, no error will occur and your bug will be fixed.

> Be careful when replaying requests using the Request Inspector – you'll need to be sure that no unexpected actions will happen.
>
> For instance, if you're debugging your application at 4 a.m. on a Sunday morning, you probably don't want to retry a request that is going to trigger a phone call to one of your customers!

Fixing common errors

Some errors in our application will be particularly common and are likely to be relatively simple to fix in most cases. This section has a quick rundown.

> You can find Twilio's full reference of error codes and their meanings at http://www.twilio.com/docs/errors/reference.

112** – HTTP errors

If Twilio has difficulties requesting TwiML from your application; for example, because your server is down, one of the error codes starting in 112 will be triggered.

These errors signify that Twilio hasn't even been able to get the TwiML from your server. Most likely, it is down, incorrectly configured, or otherwise messed up. Alternatively, the DNS records on your domain might be incorrect.

To fix this, take a look at the specifics of the error, and ideally, try placing a request yourself to see what happens.

If you're using ngrok to run your Twilio application locally, then when you restart it, you'll get a new and different URL for your applications by default, which will cause HTTP errors on the Twilio side.

To get around this, you can specify a sub domain when starting ngrok; for instance, run `ngrok -subdomain twilio-best-practices 80` and, provided it's available, you'll get `http://twilio-best-practices.ngrok.com`.

11750 – TwiML response body too large

This means that your server has responded to a request with more than 64KB of data. It's incredibly unlikely that your TwiML will be this large, and most likely, your server has responded with an HTML error page because something has gone wrong in your code.

Take a look at the request body in the Request Inspector to see what has happened.

12100 – document parse failure

Your server hasn't responded with valid XML, and thus, the response can't be valid TwiML by definition. Most likely, you've made a mistake in your TwiML or the server is responding with an error page as it did in the previous kind of error. Check the response in the Request Inspector to see what has happened.

13227 – no international authorization

You've tried to call a country that isn't enabled for your Twilio account. You can turn on and off different countries at `https://www.twilio.com/user/account/settings/international`. Check the specific case in the Request Inspector to see what country the dialed number was in.

13223-6 – phone number errors

The phone number that you tried to dial wasn't valid. Either it was completely impossible, or it was just incorrectly formatted. This usually happens where you allow users to provide phone numbers but don't validate them correctly or consistently.

You'll want to look in the Request Inspector to see the phone number that was dialed, and then you might need to make changes to your code to detect and fix such numbers or reject them entirely.

Summary

In this chapter, we covered the process of getting your application deployed and tested. When we first started building our product, we designed a flowchart that showed all of the flows and processes going on. We can then use this to ensure that we test every path through our application before deploying. Ideally, we'd do this using automated testing.

We also learned how to use Twilio's App Monitor and Triggers once our application is live to track errors, plus how to use the Request Inspector to dive deep into these errors and work out how to fix them, along with included tips on some of the most common errors.

In the next chapter, you'll find some helpful online resources that will help you get the most of this book and continue to improve your Twilio projects.

8

Online Resources

In this chapter, you'll find a short collection of online resources that will help you get the most out of this book and follow Twilio's best practices.

Hosting providers

While you're building and testing your Twilio code, you can run it on your local machine with ngrok, but once you're ready to go live, you'll need a real web hosting provider (or your own server). Here are some recommendations:

- **Heroku** (`https://www.heroku.com`): This is owned by the enterprise software powerhouse Salesforce, and specializes in making it easy to deploy and scale applications with no server expertise. It's free to start with and supports essentially every language and framework you can imagine. However, it quickly gets expensive as you scale.

- **DigitalOcean** (`https://www.digitalocean.com`): This is the fastest growing hosting provider in history, providing cheap and endlessly configurable cloud servers from $5 per month. It's an excellent platform but requires a fair bit of knowledge to configure your own server.

- **Fused** (`http://www.fused.com`): This specializes in hosting for small- and medium-sized businesses with a special focus on great customer support. You can easily host multiple applications on one account with virtually no configuration.

- **Amazon Web Services** (`http://aws.amazon.com`): This provides massively scalable hosting services on Amazon's infrastructure. If you're comfortable with server configuration, try **EC2** (`http://aws.amazon.com/ec2/`). For a solution that's easier to get started with, I'd recommend **Elastic Beanstalk** (`http://aws.amazon.com/elasticbeanstalk/`).

- **Microsoft Azure** (`http://azure.microsoft.com`): This provides scalable cloud hosting services that are particularly appropriate for those building their apps using Microsoft technologies such as .NET.

Web frameworks

Working with a framework makes it much easier to build scalable and maintainable applications compared to building everything manually.

In *Chapter 4, Twilio in the Real World*, we use the Laravel (http://laravel.com) framework to build our conferencing app. Other PHP options include **CodeIgniter** (http://www.codeigniter.com) and **CakePHP** (http://cakephp.org), both of which have strong community support. It's worth experimenting with different frameworks to see which one you like best.

Here are some recommended frameworks to play with if you're not a PHP developer:

- In Ruby, the de facto standard is **Ruby on Rails** (http://rubyonrails.org), which is a hugely popular framework with almost endless extensibility thanks to Ruby's vibrant **gems** ecosystem. It powers sites such as GitHub and Shopify.
    - ◦ If you'd prefer something more lightweight, **Sinatra** (http://www.sinatrarb.com) is the most popular choice.

- In Python, **Django** (https://www.djangoproject.com) is the most popular option, focusing on automating as much as possible, including building admin interfaces. It's used by companies such as Instagram, Pinterest, and Rdio.
    - ◦ For a more simple barebones option, **Flask** (http://flask.pocoo.org) — similar to Ruby's Sinatra — is the most used framework.

- In ASP.NET, Microsoft's own **MVC** framework (http://www.asp.net/mvc), which is bundled with the standard development tools, is used by most and is fully supported by Visual Studio.

- Working with Node.js, **Express.js** (http://expressjs.com) is most commonly used, but it is more minimalistic than the most popular frameworks in other languages. For instance, it doesn't bundle in database support.
    - ◦ Node.js is very much a developing ecosystem in web frameworks. **Koa** (http://koajs.com), **Meteor** (https://www.meteor.com), and **Hapi** (http://hapijs.com) are currently growing in popularity.

- For Java developers, **Play** (https://www.playframework.com) is the most common choice.

Automated testing

If you've never tried it before, automated testing can be a somewhat bewildering step, but it is one that makes your applications far more dependable and maintainable.

Test-driven Development (TDD) is one of the most common paradigms. Here, you write your tests before your code, make sure they fail first, and then write code to make them pass. Once this is done, you "refactor", cleaning up and reworking your code but ensuring the tests still passes.

 For a helpful general introduction to Test-driven Development, refer to `http://code.tutsplus.com/tutorials/the-newbies-guide-to-test-driven-development--net-13835`.

Now, let's look at the recommended testing libraries for the different languages and frameworks we've mentioned:

- For PHP developers, **Tuts**+ has a series of guides on TDD using PHP; refer to `http://code.tutsplus.com/series/test-driven-php--net-27482` to get started.

- For Ruby developers, the **RSpec** testing framework is a great choice. Code School has a helpful course at `https://www.codeschool.com/courses/testing-with-rspec`; you'll need to pay a monthly fee for access to much of their content, but there's a lot of great stuff there.

- For Python, the most common choice is the built-in **unittest** framework (`https://docs.python.org/3/library/unittest.html#module-unittest`) used by and recommended for the Django framework; refer to `https://docs.djangoproject.com/en/dev/topics/testing/` for details.

- The .NET Framework (and ASP.NET MVC, in particular) comes with unit testing built in with its own Unit Test framework. Refer to `http://pluralsight.com/training/Player?author=scott-allen&name=mvc4-building-m9-tests&mode=live&clip=0&course=mvc4-building` for help on getting started.

- In Node.js, the world of testing is somewhat fragmented with many options for different parts of the testing toolkit. Refer to `http://code.tutsplus.com/tutorials/testing-in-nodejs--net-35018` for a helpful primer using the **Mocha** framework.

- For Java developers, **jUnit** (`http://junit.org`) is the most commonly used option, and it can be used with frameworks such as Play; refer to `https://www.playframework.com/documentation/2.0/JavaTest` for details.

- Salesforce's Apex platform comes with its own built-in — and compulsory — testing. Refer to `https://developer.salesforce.com/page/An_Introduction_to_Apex_Code_Test_Methods` for an introduction.

Once you've written tests, it's possible to use **Continuous Integration** (CI) tools to automatically test and then even deploy your code providing the tests pass. For this, popular options include **Jenkins CI** (`http://jenkins-ci.org`), **Travis CI** (`https://travis-ci.org`), and **CircleCI** (`https://circleci.com`).

Using flowcharts

In *Chapter 7, Testing, Debugging, and Deploying Twilio Apps*, we looked at using flow charts to better plan and test our applications. Of course, you can draw these on paper, but as all developers know, a computer is always the best way!

I recommend **Draw.io** (`https://www.draw.io`), which is free and browser-based, but tools such as **Gliffy** (`http://www.gliffy.com`), **Lucidchart** (`https://www.lucidchart.com`), and the ever-popular (if expensive) **OmniGraffle** (`https://www.omnigroup.com/omnigraffle`) are great choices too.

What next?

Having read this book, you now have a great start to working with Twilio. However, where should you go next to keep learning? Take a look:

- The Twilio documentation is very complete and includes full details on all of Twilio's different APIs and libraries. You can start exploring them at `http://www.twilio.com/docs`.

- The Twilio Blog at `https://www.twilio.com/blog/` frequently posts ideas for projects, help with using new Twilio features, and even general programming advice. It's a great place to follow, if only for inspiration.

- If you ever have any difficulties with Twilio, try asking for help on Stack Overflow at `http://stackoverflow.com/questions/tagged/twilio`. A fair few Twilio staff are often there to help out!

Index

N

Nginx
 URL, for HTTP Basic Authentication 134
ngrok
 about 10, 32
 URL 32, 149
 used, for testing Twilio application 32
 used, for testing Twilio application on
  Linux 33, 34
 used, for testing Twilio application on Mac
  OS X 33, 34
 used, for testing Twilio application on
  Windows 33
Node.js library
 installing 127
 URL, for documentation 128
nouns 7, 13
npm 127
NuGet
 URL 125

O

OmniGraffle
 URL 154
outgoing caller IDs
 about 64
 URL 65
outgoing calls
 handling, for power 75
 handling, for security 75
 placing, with Twilio Client 75, 76

P

package manager
 used, for downloading Twilio PHP
  library 48
parameters, phone numbers
 Contains 63
 InRegion 63
 SmsEnabled 63
parameters, Twilio's requests
 ApiVersion 11
 Body 12
 CallerName 12

 CallSid/MessageSid 11
 CallStatus 11
 Direction 11
 ForwardedFrom 11
 From 11
 From/To 12
 To 11
Parsley
 about 96
 URL 96
phone numbers
 outgoing caller IDs 65
 short codes 65
 working with 62, 63
phone numbers, resources
 AvailablePhoneNumber 62
 IncomingPhoneNumber 62
 OutgoingCallerId 62
 ShortCode 62
PHP library
 about 122
 installing 122
 URL, for documentation 122
pip
 URL, for installation 124
 using 124
Play
 URL 152
POODLE
 about 136
 reference link 136
Postman
 about 40, 50
 parameters, sending to requests 52
 requests, making 50, 51
 requests, tracking with Collections 53-55
 requests, tracking with History 53-55
 URL, for downloading 50
POST request, parameters
 ApplicationSid 55
 Body 59
 From 55, 59
 reference link 56
 To 55, 59
 Url 55
Public Switched Telephone
  Network (PSTN) 73

Thank you for buying
Twilio Best Practices

About Packt Publishing

Packt, pronounced 'packed', published its first book, *Mastering phpMyAdmin for Effective MySQL Management*, in April 2004, and subsequently continued to specialize in publishing highly focused books on specific technologies and solutions.

Our books and publications share the experiences of your fellow IT professionals in adapting and customizing today's systems, applications, and frameworks. Our solution-based books give you the knowledge and power to customize the software and technologies you're using to get the job done. Packt books are more specific and less general than the IT books you have seen in the past. Our unique business model allows us to bring you more focused information, giving you more of what you need to know, and less of what you don't.

Packt is a modern yet unique publishing company that focuses on producing quality, cutting-edge books for communities of developers, administrators, and newbies alike. For more information, please visit our website at www.packtpub.com.

About Packt Open Source

In 2010, Packt launched two new brands, Packt Open Source and Packt Enterprise, in order to continue its focus on specialization. This book is part of the Packt Open Source brand, home to books published on software built around open source licenses, and offering information to anybody from advanced developers to budding web designers. The Open Source brand also runs Packt's Open Source Royalty Scheme, by which Packt gives a royalty to each open source project about whose software a book is sold.

Writing for Packt

We welcome all inquiries from people who are interested in authoring. Book proposals should be sent to author@packtpub.com. If your book idea is still at an early stage and you would like to discuss it first before writing a formal book proposal, then please contact us; one of our commissioning editors will get in touch with you.

We're not just looking for published authors; if you have strong technical skills but no writing experience, our experienced editors can help you develop a writing career, or simply get some additional reward for your expertise.

Twilio Cookbook
Second Edition

ISBN: 978-1-78355-065-4   Paperback: 334 pages

Over 70 easy-to-follow recipes, from exploring the key features of Twilio to building advanced telephony apps

1. Updated to include picture messaging, call queueing, and Twilio Client; all recommended by Twilio.

2. The only book that teaches you how to set up your own conference calling system or how to build a PBX for your company.

3. Each recipe is a carefully organized sequence of instructions to complete the task as efficiently as possible.

Twilio Cookbook

ISBN: 978-1-78216-606-1   Paperback: 266 pages

Over 60 easy-to-follow recipes ranging from walking you through key features of Twilio's API to building advanced telephony applications

1. Teaches software developers to programmatically make and receive phone calls and send and receive text messages using Twilio's web service APIs.

2. The only book that teaches you how to set up your own conference calling system or how to build a PBX for your company, or how to build a local solution that can tell you the weather where you are.

Please check **www.PacktPub.com** for information on our titles

Learning Xamarin Studio

ISBN: 978-1-78355-081-4   Paperback: 248 pages

Learn how to build high-performance native applications using the power of Xamarin Studio

1. Get a full introduction to the key features and components of the Xamarin 3 IDE and framework, including Xamarin.Forms and iOS visual designer.

2. Install, integrate, and utilise Xamarin Studio with the tools required for building amazing cross-platform applications for iOS and Android.

3. Create, test, and, deploy apps for your business and for the app store.

JMeter Cookbook

ISBN: 978-1-78398-828-0   Paperback: 228 pages

70 insightful and practical recipes to help you successfully use Apache JMeter

1. Leverage existing cloud services for distributed testing and learn to employ your own cloud infrastructure when needed.

2. Successfully integrate JMeter into your continuous delivery workflow allowing you to deliver high quality products.

3. Test application supporting services and resources including RESTful, SOAP, JMS, FTP, and Database.

www.ingramcontent.com/pod-product-compliance
Lightning Source LLC
Chambersburg PA
CBHW060135060326
40690CB00018B/3893